Father and Child: Community College Achievement Based on African-American Family Structure

By A'lon Michael Holliday

ISBN: 978-1-7353744-0-6

This book is protected by the copyright laws of the United States of America. This book may not be copied or reprinted for commercial gain or profit. No part of this publication may be reproduced, distributed, or transmitted in any form or by any means or stored in a database or retrieval system without prior written permission of the Publisher.

Copyright ©2020 Michael Holliday

All rights reserved, including the right to reproduce this book or portion thereof in any form whatsoever.

Table of Contents

Table of Contents iii
Dedication i
Acknowledgements ii
Abstract iv
Preface vi
Foreword x
Introduction xii
CHAPTER 1: Looking at the African-American Family Structure ... 1
CHAPTER 2: The Researchers Weigh In on the Family Structure 29
CHAPTER 3: The Sample of Students Studied 65
Table 3.1 Second Year Status 67
CHAPTER 4: The Present Study's Family Structure Findings 73
Table 4.1 Participants 79
Table 4.2 Dimensions, Themes, Patterns, and Discrepancies 130
Table 4.3 Patterns Emerging across Dimensions 134
CHAPTER 5: Study Conclusions and Recommendations 135
References 157
About the Author 165

Dedication

I would like to dedicate this to Herbert Lawrence Jr., my father and the person who shared his passion and experiences that gave me strength in my hardest times. This is also dedicated to my daughter, Siena, my inspiration and greatest achievement.

Acknowledgements

"There's two types of parents in this world, A'lon: Selfish parents and unselfish parents. I have given you all that I have."

– Marguerite Holliday

My mom would tell me this when I would want the new bomber jacket or new Adidas sneakers. She worked, borrowed, and begged (thank God for layaway) to provide for me. Because of your unwavering support I succeeded and because of your unconditional love I overcame every obstacle.

From LaSalle Military Academy in New York to Boston College you made sure I soared with eagles. Through law school and, finally, my doctorate at Dowling College in New York, you were always my biggest supporter.

I wish I listened in my early years when you talked about things. But your words built a bridge that has steadily supported every step I have taken.

Thank you, Mom.

Love always, your son, A'lon

I would like to thank my mother for her unwavering support through this process; my family for its support and understanding; Dr. Stephanie Tatum, Dowling College Chair of Dissertation Committee Department of Leadership, Technology, and Education, for sharing her knowledge and patience; and my dissertation committee members, Dr. Kevin Jordan, Dowling College professor, Department of Leadership, Technology, and Education; Dr. Walter , Dowling College professor, Department of Leadership, Technology, and Education; Dr. Elsa Sofia Morote, Dowling College professor, Department of Leadership, Technology, and Education; and Dr. Richard Bernato, Dowling College professor, Department of Leadership, Technology, and Education for their contribution to this dissertation and to my maturation.

Abstract

Despite the growing body of research on African-American students' academic achievement and the role mothers play in their child's academic development, few studies (Carter, 2008; Fordham, 1988) examined the role fathers play in the development of their child's academic achievement. The primary aim of this study was to examine how the father or male surrogate influences the development of six dimensions: personal identity, social sensitivity, academic self-concept, resilience, race theory, and vision of own success. Sixteen second-year community college students in New York were interviewed--nine males and seven females. The semi-structured interview protocol questions were developed based on the research literature regarding the six dimensions. The results indicated differences between academically successful students with a father or male surrogate and academically unsuccessful students without a father or male surrogate. The father or male surrogate contributed positively to the development of the six dimensions, and the absence of a father or male surrogate contributed to a lack of confidence, direction, and the inability to see past negative stereotypical labels given by the media and instructors.

Preface

I imagined myself a Dr. Huxtable, just like in the TV show. I would have a wonderful complete family, a great job, a wife, a child, a dog, and a beautiful home in Brooklyn Heights or Long Island. We would raise our child together happily ever after. We would have everything that I didn't have growing up. I lived in a household where my mom was re-married, and I never heard from my biological father until I was told he died. I never prepared to parent alone and I didn't know what I would bring to a child's life that was valuable as a father. Through my own father I was shown that my mother would take care of everything I wanted and needed. Little boy lessons to young adult lessons--she had it covered.

When I divorced my daughter's mother the reality set in that despite my willingness and eagerness to become a father, fathers were viewed by some as not important as the mother. The Family Court system, public opinion, and even the woman I shared a child with had the same view, ironically. I would be lying if I said I didn't begin to believe this--I was a product of this myself, right? Through the Family Court system fathers are baptized with phrases like "primary care taker, custodial parent, and parental time." Fathering almost becomes a "thing," a moveable part that can be replaced or subtracted at any time without any measurable consequence, or so we are told. How many times do we hear about African-American households being run by a single mother or depictions of single mothers on television and movies? This is our reality, right? We put on the mask and pretend it's OK, but inside it's not. We have questions and need answers, but pride and ego take the wheel and steer. So many of us resign, raise the white flag and, in some cases, disappear.

As I was constantly being compared to fathers who abandoned their responsibilities as a parent, I was considered an outlier. I was told, "You're not like other fathers, you're different, and the court and public opinion go with what they see as the "norm." What can I do? Is this worth even fighting for? How can I show the world why my involvement is important? I didn't want to be a "curb-side pickup" dad or a "holiday day" or a "weekend father." It was such an isolating feeling because I didn't think anyone was going through the same feeling and experiences that I had. Frankly, most African-American fathers don't share their battle stories with each other.

So, I buried myself in pursuing my doctorate and fighting for the right to raise my daughter, trying to convince a judge who never walked in my shoes or experienced the life of an African-American father that my impact and influence is just as important as the mother's. And then do battle with your child's legal guardian who tries to assess the importance of your 2-year-old's opinion of you in her life. I researched and researched and researched to find nothing remotely close by literary scholars who researched African- American fathers and their impact on their children. I created my own philosophy that the father and mother raise the daughter; the daughter watches how the father treats the mother; and then the daughter picks a partner similar to her father to marry and start a family. The cycle continues over and over. The father is needed--we have to be around or the daughter doesn't have an example of whom to marry. In my mind, this was gold. I just couldn't find any research that demonstrated that the father's impact was significant. I once said, "If you watch celebrities win awards, they thank God and moms, but rarely dads." We are almost conditioned to believe the father bears no responsibility or impact. I knew I had to change this, and I knew I wasn't the only father feeling this way.

Many times I wanted to give up fighting for my rights in court, and let the system decide what's best for my daughter and control my worth. But I knew there was something deeper in developing my rights as a father, and it was showing the impact fathers have on their children, not just as adolescents but as young adults. So it led me to define what a father really is. This is key because many men accept the role of father but are never given the title.

My research challenged the thought that academic success is the only way a father can contribute to children. Terms such as social identity, resilience, and academic self-concept are used to provide a look into the important variables fathers instill in their children.

Though I may have not become a Huxtable, through this process I became something greater--a father who knows his worth.

Foreword

Being an African-American single father and being very active in my daughter's life (academically and in social development), I discussed a lot of the obstacles (good and bad) I faced with other single fathers. The pathological view that African-American fathers did not take an active role in their children's life weighed heavy on me. I knew first-hand that this couldn't be true. I have a lot of friends, family members, and colleagues that proved this wrong. TV, empirical studies, movies, and news never showed positive images of African-American fatherhood. When I first suggested my topic for my dissertation at the Dowling College School of Leadership, Technology and Education Program I was told by one professor that this topic "will make you no money and frankly no one cares." This pushed me even more to do it! In 2008 I began the three-year process of understanding what a dissertation is and the complex research that goes into it. Under the guidance of my chair, Dr. Stephanie Tatum, I was able to develop my title and abstract.

This would embody the idea of what and how a father impacts his child's life socially and academically. Personal identity, social sensitivity, academic self-concept, resilience, race theory, and vision of own success are all variables that a father presence can impact and in my finding does. I interviewed 16 second-year community college students in New York. With the assistance of the Director of the Black Male Initiative there I had a pool of students. The findings were astonishing and revealing. I was awarded my doctorate degree in Leadership, Technology, and Education in 2011 from Dowling College, holding my daughter in my left arm and holding diploma in my right.

Introduction

Despite the growing body of research on African-American students' academic achievement and the role mothers play in their child's academic development, few studies have examined the role fathers play in the development of their child's academic achievement. The primary aim of this study was to examine how the father or male surrogate influences the development of six dimensions: personal identity, social sensitivity, academic self-concept, resilience, race theory, and vision of own success. Sixteen second-year community college students in New York were interviewed: nine males and seven females. The semi-structured interview protocol questions were developed based on the research literature regarding the six dimensions. The results indicated differences between academically successful students with a father or male surrogate and academically unsuccessful students without a father or male surrogate. The father or male surrogate contributed positively to the development of the six dimensions, and the absence of a father or male surrogate caused a lack of confidence, direction, and the inability to see past negative stereotypes that they are labeled with by the media or instructors they encounter.

CHAPTER 1: Looking at the African-American Family Structure

The African-American family structure comes into question in a wide range of research that discusses African-American students' academic achievement, implicating the family as one of the reasons for the decline in African-American educational attainment. The family structure has been depicted as broken and the reason for the decline in the success of African-American students.

One expert, Joyce Aschenbrenner, states, "The assumption still appears that African-Americans are incomplete or are characterized as an unorthodox version of the U.S. family." The depiction of African-American families on television and negative portrayal of slavery in classroom history books focus on alleged weaknesses, pathologies, its matriarchal form, instability, and lack of productivity. The impression, then, is that these are the characteristics of most African-American families. Joyce Aschenberger in a 1973 study, "Extended Families among Black Americans," in the *Journal of Comparative Studies* concludes that the portrayal of the African-American family generally does not include intact family structures, whereby there is stability and both parents are engaged in the child's life.

Researcher Robert B. Hill, who wrote *Strength of Black Families*, examined statistical analyses the U.S. Census Bureau generated regarding African-American families and found five strengths inherent in their family structures: strong kinship bonds, work orientation, adaptability of family roles, high achievement orientation, and religious orientation. Inherent in these strengths is the ability to adapt to circumstances, which is critical for survival and advancement in a sometimes hostile environment.

The first strength of African-American families is strong kinship bonds. Hill states, "The census Bureau statistics reveal that Black families are far more likely than White ones to absorb younger related family members." The community bond that develops among African-American families is stronger than reported. They support each other and recognize if a member of the community is having any hardships. In some instances, African-American family structure may include non-biological members living in or out of the home called fictive kinship. Fictive kinship is the practice of creating a family bond between people who are not related by blood, researcher Orlando Patterson notes in *Slavery and Social Death: a Comparative Study* by Harvard University Press, which was practiced by slaves, who were often separated from their biological family members, as well as used on a normal basis to define the bonds between close friends. It is sometimes a coping mechanism for when your own family members are non-existent or non-functional.

The second strength identified by Hill is a strong work orientation. Hill explains:

> Three-fifths of the Black poor hold jobs as compared to one half of the white poor. Three-fifths of Black families are headed by women who work, though more than 60 percent of them are classified as poor, and about half receive welfare assistance.

In the area of job stability, blacks record a longer employment than whites do. Hill further notes that

> According to some studies conducted in 1967 to 1971, some 20 percent more Blacks than Whites held current jobs for three years or more, and almost half of the Blacks, compared to a third of the Whites, held their jobs for ten or more years.

The third strength Hill discusses is the adaptability of family roles. He states, "There is a sharing of decisions and jobs in the home, and when unanticipated separation occurs, this role flexibility tends to act as a stabilizing factor…. Most Black families with two parents have an equalitarian pattern." Hill brings about the idea that black families may have a household with a dominant female presence; it functions under a sharing of jobs, responsibilities, and decisions.

A fourth major strength of the black family is its high achievement orientation. Hill's research shows that, "About 80 percent of Blacks entering college today come from homes in which the father did not attend college, meaning that poor Blacks are entering college in unprecedented numbers." What can be inferred from Hill's research is that African-Americans who fit the census guidelines for the category of a lower economic status were more economically stable and more academically successful than whites in the same socioeconomic status.

The fifth and last major source of black family strength is religious orientation. Hill explains: "Since slavery, Black families have utilized religion as a haven, a shield, and a source of rebellion, but above all as a survival mechanism." The erroneous idea that black families are plagued by abandonment issues is also addressed by Hill when he argues that "This has been greatly over estimated. Actually about a fifth of Black families in 1969 come under of the category of 'deserted' in figures released on aid to deserted families in the United States."

Jaleel Abdul-Adil and Alvin David Farmer Jr. demonstrate in "Inner City African- American Parental Involvement in Elementary Schools: Getting beyond Urban Legends of Apathy" how Hill's work is still relevant through identifying current pathologies about the African-American family structure. Abdul and Farmer state Desimone analyzed parent and student surveys from the National Education Longitudinal Study of 1988 and found that African- American parents reported lower overall rates of parental involvement across a range of different activities in comparison to their European American counterparts. These low reported rates of inner-city African- American parental involvement persisted even in selected cases where their children were classified as academically gifted. These results suggest that inner-city African-American parents may be disinterested in (and possibly hostile to) their children's educational success. Consequently, an "urban legend" of apathy has emerged among disappointed and often frustrated researchers and professionals that inner-city African-American parental involvement is an extremely difficult, or even impossible, task according to the Laura Desimone 1999 study, "Linking Parent Involvement with Student Achievement: Do Race and Income Matter?"

Broader frameworks may be necessary to accurately detect and depict inner-city African-American parental involvement. For example, DeMoss and Vaughn conducted a phenomenological study of 26 actively involved African-American parents who participated in school-related activities. The involved parents participated in multiple ways in their own and other children's lives both inside and outside schools, such as attending events, monitoring homework, etc. The researchers concluded that involved parents in predominantly inner-city African-American communities have more frequent rates and diverse types of participation than are commonly detected by or portrayed in the mainstream research.

Aschenberger conducted research that identified five types of households with several ethnic backgrounds. The family structures she identified were:

> (1) conjugal-nuclear which consist of the husband, wife, and unmarried children; (2) conjugal-extended, which consists of parents and unmarried or separated sons and daughters and their children; (3) matrifocal–nuclear consisting of a mother and young children; (4) matrifocal--extended, which consists of mother and unmarried or separated daughters and their children; and (5) single men residing alone. The primary difference of a matrifocal and conjugal household is the presence of an adult male as husband and father on a permanent basis.

In her research, Aschenberger includes African-American families and explains the different structures that embody them. Aschenberger's research did not discuss the effect the father's presence has on the academic achievement of the children. Skowron examined differentiation of self and defined it as "the capacity of a system and its members to manage emotional reactivity, act thoughtfully under stress, and allow for both intimacy and autonomy in relationships." Elizabeth Skowron in a 2005 study, "Parent Differentiation of Self and Child Competence in Low-income Urban Families" used a sample of "low income urban families in order to explore the relative importance of parent differentiation versus environmental stress for predicting competence in children."

Skowron concluded that,

> The mother's capacity to regulate emotionality was also significantly associated with child academic and pro social behavior...low income urban families with mothers who are more differentiated had children who demonstrated stronger verbal and math problem-solving skills and were less aggressive.

The family structure in the African-American family home plays a role in the academic achievement of the child. A parent's impact on a student's vision of success is great. Skowron mentions that the mother's influence on the academic achievement can lead to strong verbal and math success. The presence of the parent can influence goal creation and attainment.

Researcher Nancy Boyd-Franklin noted in her book *A Psycho-educational Perspective on Black Parenting* in 1985 that African-American fathers were frequently seen as men who were not active and had little power, control, or interest in the socialization of their children. Deborah Johnson's book *Father Presence Matters: a Review of Literature from the National Center of Fathers and Families* in 1996 identified the parental influence on the academic achievement of African-American students. She states, "Studies of father absence have identified children's behavioral, academic, and social problems, each with unique features linked to their developmental stages." A major focus on a father's absence has been its effect on the intellectual and school performance of children. Children in father-absent households had lower IQ, verbal, and performance scores than children in father-present households, according to the research of Elise Lessing, Susan Zagorin, and Dorothy Nelson in a 1970 book, *WISC Subtest and IQ Scores Correlates of Fathers' Absences*. Maxine Thompson, Karl Alexander, and Doris Entwisle in 1988 research in the book *Household Composition, Parental Expectations and School Achievement* looked at Milne's 1986 study that found children living with one parent performed less well than children in a two-parent household on reading and vocabulary and on verbal and standardized exams.

    The parental contribution to the character an academically successful student acquires plays a pivotal role in their development from childhood to adulthood. An African-American student must be able to work hard academically but also hurdle obstacles that they encounter: negative stereotypes by instructors and classmates. Achievement of African-American students has been attributed to hard work and strong work habits by researcher Dorinda Carter's study "Achievement as Resistance: the Development of a Critical Race Achievement Ideology among Black Achievers" in the *Harvard Educational Review* in 2008. Work habits have been associated with a parental influence in a high achieving student's life, that study argued.

John Ogbu research in his book *Schooling in the Ghetto* stated in 1981 that black parents instill in their children a belief in education. This forms a student's academic self-concept, which is the perception that students have about themselves regarding their academic performance, abilities and achievement, according to Herbert Marsh & Rosalie Oneill's book *Self-Description Questionnaire* in 1984. A parent's involvement has been linked to the development of a student's academic self-concept as well as their environment John Ogbu concluded in a 2004 book, *Collective Identity and the Burden of 'Acting White.'* A parent provides a student the ability to walk into a classroom and feel he or she can compete at any level with any student regardless of his or her race. However, navigating through the different ethnic groups they may come into contact with in school requires an ability to balance between their home life and school life.

Dorinda Carter's 2008 study examined nine high achieving African-American students and the characteristics and coping mechanism they developed that enabled them to successfully navigate a predominantly white high school. Her findings suggested that academically successful African-American students sustain school success by embodying African-American pride and realizing how race may play a pivotal role in hampering their success. She states, "Students do not maintain school success by simply having a strong racial self-concept or a strong achievement self-concept; rather, they discuss achieving in the context of being Black or African-American." For these students, being a black or African-American achiever in a predominantly white high school means embodying racial group pride, as well as having a critical understanding of how race and racism operate to potentially constrain one's success.

Similar to other studies about high academic achieving students Anysia Mayer in 2008's *Expanding Opportunities for High Academic Achievement* and Michael Cunningham, Megan Hurley, and Dana Foney in a 2002 book, *Influence of Perceived Contextual Stress on Self-esteem and Academic Outcomes in African-American Adolescents,* do not mention the father's role or the specific characteristics and coping mechanism used to achieve academically in a predominantly white educational institution. The student is given the credit for developing these coping practices. Carter's year-long 2008 qualitative study, investigating the adaptive behavior African-American students developed to navigate through a predominantly white high school, identified six dimensions. In order to examine similarities and differences in experience and adaptive behavior, she interviewed nine high achieving African-American students individually and later brought them together in a focus group. Students identified six dimensions that were critical in maintaining academic success: Students must be able to balance between their school environment and maintain cultural identity, have the ability to overcome racial obstacles such as negative stereotypes by classmates and instructors, believe that they have the skills and resources to succeed, understand that racism exists and it will not prevent their success, and have a positive perception of their academic abilities.

Carter in 2008 found that high achieving African-American students develop resilient and adaptive behaviors that allow them to successfully achieve in a racially hostile environment. Carter concludes that these students are able to develop these adaptive behaviors without losing their racial identification. Specifically, African-American high achievers enrolled in predominantly white schools were able to achieve academically by developing certain skills that would help them achieve despite racial tension in and out of the classroom. Through her research, she was able to identify characteristics of African-American students who achieved academically in an all-white suburban environment. Carter noted that if a critical race achievement ideology was adopted in educational institutions it would lead to student success. She states, "the maintenance and development of this type of ideology in black students--particularly those who are being educated in predominantly white school contexts--can foster positive attitudes and beliefs about schooling and adaptive behaviors for success." This aligns with the vision of success defined in this research by demonstrating the impact the school environment plays on their vision of what success is.

African-American high achieving students view achievement as a human race-less character trait embedded in their sense of self as a racial being, Carter notes. The alignment of achievement beliefs, attitudes, and behaviors is nurtured in many ways. Many high achieving African-American students possess strong racial and ethnic self-concepts; positive racial socialization allows them to view themselves as successful. This high racial centrality and positive racial regard is nurtured by a counter-narrative conveyed by parents who emphasize pride and self-respect as members of the racial group, Theresa Perry concluded in her 2003 research "Achieving in Post-civil rights America."

The research literature on high achieving African-American students presents a variety of constructs that influence student success such as personal identity, academic self-concept, critical race theory, cultural codes, resiliency, and a vision of success that they want for themselves. The prospect of an association between a high achieving African-American student and a parent present or a male surrogate influence could lead to a better understanding of the exact role a father plays in the academic success of a student and could provide valuable information on what could be done to support this relationship between the father and student. Specifically, the role of the African-American father in the development of a successful son or daughter in a community college has not been well investigated and needs to be examined further. The specific role of the African-American father in the academic achievement of his child has not been well documented and, in many cases, the African-American father has been described as having little interest in his children's academic achievement, according to a 1985 study, "A Psycho-educational Perspective on Black Parenting," by Nancy Boyd-Franklin.

Purpose of the Study

The six dimensions that Carter identified in her study were used to describe what high academic-achieving African-American students use to maintain academic achievement and cultural identification and how presence or lack of a father or male surrogate influences each dimension: personal identity, social sensitivity, academic self-concept, resilience, race theory, and vision of own success. The purpose of this study was to investigate how African-American sons and daughters who have a father presence at home, or who have a male surrogate available, and who do not have a father presence at home or male surrogate available develop their own race theory, personal identity, social sensitivities, resiliency, academic self-concept, and a vision for their own success. Furthermore, these African-American sons and daughters will be examined by their successful and non-successful achievement of second-year status in a community college.

The Problem

How do African-American sons and daughters in a community college with or without a father or a male surrogate present describe their personal identity, academic self-concept, their race theory, social sensitivity, resiliency, and a vision for their own success? Furthermore, when they are compared and contrasted as academically successful or unsuccessful in their second year of community college, what are the similarities and differences in their personal identity, academic self-concept, their race theory, social sensitivity, resiliency, and a vision for their own success?

The following research questions guided this study:

Question One

How do academically successful and unsuccessful African-American sons and daughters who have second-year status in a community college with or without a father or male surrogate present describe their personal identity?

Question Two

How do academically successful and unsuccessful African-American sons and daughters who have second-year status in a community college with or without a father or male surrogate present describe their academic self-concept?

Question Three

How do academically successful and unsuccessful African-American sons and daughters who have second-year status in a community college with or without a father or male surrogate present describe their own race theory?

Question Four

How do academically successful and unsuccessful African-American sons and daughters who have second-year status in a community college with or without a father or male surrogate present describe their social sensitivity?

Question Five

How do academically successful and unsuccessful African-American sons and daughters who have second-year status in a community college with or without a father or male surrogate present describe their resiliency?

Question Six

How do academically successful and unsuccessful African-American sons and daughters who have second-year status in a community college with or without a father or male surrogate present describe their vision of success?

Definition of Major Variables and Terms

Father

For the purpose of this study, a father is operationally defined as a natural father present in the home on almost a daily basis.

Male Surrogate

A male role model is involved in the student's life as a stepfather, other relative, or fictive kinship who provides regular contact with the student on a daily basis. A relationship, based not on blood or marriage but rather on religious rituals, such as attending church and gathering to demonstrate faith-based occasions or close friendships that replicates many of the rights and obligations usually associated with family, as defined by Mary Curry and Helen Rose Ebaugh's research "Fictive Kin as Social Capital in New Immigrant Communities" in 2000.

No Male Surrogate

A male rarely or not involved at all in the student's life.

Critical Race Theory

Critical Race Theory provides explanations for the experiences African-Americans have in social institutions, including education, for the purposes of eliminating social stratification through social justice. However, unlike traditional civil rights, which embrace incrementalism and step-by-step progress, Critical Race Theory questions the very foundations of the liberal order, including equality theory, legal reasoning, enlightened rationalism, and neutral principles of constitutional law, as defined by Richard Delgado and Jean Stefancic's research "Critical Race Theory" in 2001. Critical Race Theory takes some of the civil rights principles established and uses them to create awareness of the injustices and discrimination African-Americans encounter in numerous areas in life. The goal in Critical Race Theory is to change the practices and laws that inhibit the understanding and growth of African-Americans.

Personal Identity

One's positive self-identification or personal identity is necessary to sustain school success. For such an identification to form and persist, one must perceive that one has the skills and resources to prosper, according to John Ogbu and Signithia Fordham's *Black Students' Schools Success Coping with the Burden of 'Acting White.'*

Social Sensitivity

Social sensitivity is the ability to move within and between various sub-cultures and to understand the utility of acquiring the cultural capital of various cultural formations including characteristics of success, as noted by Concha Delgado-Gaitan and Enrique T. Trueba in 1991's research "Crossing Cultural Borders: Education for Immigration Families in America."

Resiliency

Resilience is the development and implementation of strategies for dealing with racism in and out of the classroom and non-classroom domain. It is also defined as a student's ability to resist, persevere, and develop coping mechanisms in a harsh learning environment crucial key to one's academic success, according to Tracy Robinson and Janice Victoria Ward in 1991.

Academic Self-Concept

Academic Self-Concept is the perception that students have about themselves regarding their academic performance, abilities and achievement, argue Herbert Marsh and Rosalie Oneill in their 1984 research "Self-Description Questionnaire : the construct Validity of Multi-dimensional Self-Concept Rating by Late Adolescents."

Academically Successful Community College Student

Students enrolled full time in their second year of college, have a grade point average of 3.0 or better, and have obtained 30 credits or more and currently enrolled in an advanced placement program, according to Wayne S.Obetz's 1987 research book, *A Proposed Model for Categorizing Successful and Non-successful Student Outcomes.*

Academically Unsuccessful Community College Student

Students enrolled full time in their second year of college, have a grade point average of 2.0 or obtained less than 30 credits, and currently registered in a remedial program, as defined by Wayne S. Obetz.

Vision of Success

Vision of success is a personal depiction of the future. He or she considers success as obtaining financial stability, achieving specific career aspirations, and graduating from college, Dorinda Carter argued in a 2008 study.

Conceptual Rationale

Hill identifies five strengths that many African-American families use in navigating through hostile environments. The five strengths are kinship bonds, strong work orientation, adaptability of family roles, high achievement orientation, and religious orientation. He uses statistical data gathered by the U.S. Census Bureau to demonstrate the inaccurate depiction of the African-American family structure and, in turn, shows the strengths that have been overlooked. Susan DeMoss and CourtneyVaughn in

2000's research work "Reflections on Theory and Practice in Parent Involvement from a Phenomenological Perspective" conducted a phenomenological study of 26 actively involved African-American parents who participated in school-related activities. The involved parents participated in multiple ways in their own and other children's lives both inside and outside schools (e.g., attending events, monitoring homework, etc.). The researchers concluded that involved parents in predominantly inner-city African-American communities have more frequent rates and diverse types of participation than are commonly detected by or portrayed in the mainstream research. Jaleel Abdul-Adil and Alvin David Farmer Jr. in 2006 demonstrated how Robert B. Hill's 1972 work, *Strength of Black Families* is still relevant through identifying current pathologies about the African-American family structure. Consequently, an "urban legend" of apathy has emerged among disappointed and often frustrated researchers and professionals that inner-city African-American parental involvement is an extremely difficult, or even impossible, task.

Wynona Bryant-Williams and Ronald Fannin in 1996 discussed in *Middle Class African-American Perceptions Regarding Their Strengths* the traditional approach to understanding African- American family structures, which has been to depict the family in a very negative way. They state, "A content analysis of

10 key journals in sociology and social work revealed that articles on African-American comprised only 3 percent of 3,547 empirical studies of American families published between 1965 and 1975." The result of Bryant-Williams and Fannin's study indicates that African-American families hold in high regard the same values, morals and principles as families of other ethnic groups. They are dedicated to maintaining stable families, having high expectations for their children as well as for themselves, and are involved with community and civic organizations, which promotes the improvements of African-Americans.

The father's role, however, is not clearly defined and, in many instances, he is omitted. Nancy Boy-Franklin's *Psycho-educational Perspectives on Black Parenting* in 1985 stated that the father has been looked at as being non-existent in the social development of his children and, in many instances, he has been seen as having no interest. However, John Lewis McAdoo's book *The roles of African-American Fathers in the Socialization of the Children* conducted a study in 1979 in Maryland that examined the components of the father-child interaction process and the relationship of the development and social competence in African-American preschool children. The results revealed that a great deal of interaction occurred between the father and child.

Sadiye Logan's research "Fathers Are Nurturers" in 1983 also identified the role of African-American fathers in the home. Logan concluded that all the fathers viewed nurturance as an important, highly valued dimension of their role and self-identity. Jennifer Hammer's *The Fathers of Fatherless Black Children* in 1997 conducted a qualitative study of roles of African-American fathers by exploring their perspective on fatherhood. Primarily, they insisted that spending time with their children was their most essential fatherhood function, regardless of how much money they were able to provide for their children's well-being. The subjects indicated that a man's presence, his love, and his affection were essential for the optimal rearing of a child.

The development of a child's ability to believe he or she can achieve academically may come from the impact of family, student, and school characteristics. Locus of control is a term in psychology that refers to a person's belief about what causes the good or bad results in his or her life and how they internalize and externalize these results. If one intends to estimate the influence of locus of control on African-American students' educational aspirations, three sets of control variables must be taken into account: family characteristics, student characteristics, and school characteristics, according to researchers. Lamont Flowers, Richard Miler and James L. Moore III's 2003 study "Effects of Locus of Control in African-America High School Seniors'

Educational Aspirations" investigated that impact. The results of the study suggest that African-American high school seniors who reported higher levels of locus of control were more likely to have higher educational aspirations than African-American high school seniors who reported lower levels of locus of control.

The dimensions of this research are addressed by six major theoretical underpinnings as defined by researchers: critical race theory, vision of success, social sensitivity, academic self-concept, resiliency, and personal identity. However, each theorist does not explore the relationship between the academically successful or unsuccessful African-American student and the influence of having a father may have on these dimensions. Richard Delgado and Jean Stefancic in their 1995 study discuss in their book *Critical Race Theory* that it is a collection of activist and scholars interested in studying and transforming the relationship among race, racism, and power; yet, they do not focus on the core relationship between the father and his children.

Concha Delgado-Gaitan and Henry Trueba's research crossing cultural borders in 1991 discussed social sensitivity as the ability of one to move within and between various sub-cultures and to understand the utility of acquiring the cultural capitol of various cultural formations, including success. Although, Delgado-Gaitan and Trueba discuss how African-American students use this ability to achieve academically in school, they do not identify if family members, specifically fathers, influence this dimension.

Rosyln Mickelson in a 1990 study, "Black Working Class Attitudes toward Academic Achievement," defines resiliency as developing strategies for dealing with racism in and out of the classroom that reflect varying degrees of resistance. Mickelson examines how the student develops resiliency and how he or she uses this to navigate in a hostile school environment. The development of resiliency is not only developed and taught through experience but through modeling as well. The parental structure a child experiences and the community influences may contribute to the development of resiliency.

Richard Shavelson, Judith Hubner, and George Stanton's work "Self-concept and Validation of Construct Interpretations" in 1976 stated that academic self-concept determines how you compare yourself academically to other students. Though there has been an increased amount of research on academic self concept, determining the African-American's father's contribution to his child's academic self-concept has not been examined at the rate of a mother's contribution. In fact, much of the literature focuses on the mother's contribution.

John Ogbu and Dorinda Carter define vision of success as the achievement of a desired outcome related to an individual's quality of life, such as completing high school, entering college, or owning a business. This particular dimension will help establish where students develop their goals and how much of an impact a father has or may not have on that development. This could be beneficial in determining whether a father's own vision of success influences his children's.

There is a dearth of research literature on an academically successful and unsuccessful African-American college student's relationship with his or her father. The current study will examine the father's role on his child's academic achievement. In particular, the development of specific dimensions influenced by the father or male surrogate may contribute to academic success.

This research intends to examine a father's role in the social, emotional, and academic development of his children and his influence on the development of their personal identity, critical race theory, social sensitivities, academic self-concept, resiliency, and vision of success. It seeks to provide information on whether or not fathers contribute to the racial ideology and resilience many African-American students need to navigate successfully in American educational institutions. The need to understand this contribution can provide insight for community and educational leaders on the importance of the presence of African- American fathers or male surrogate.

Significance of the Study

This study has the potential to help educators better understand the nuanced relationship between African-American fathers and their children. They will have a better understanding between the effect a father's role has on their academic experience and perception, as well as explore the influence the father has on achievement ideology and school behaviors of high achieving African-American college students across the six dimensions. In particular, it will also analyze how African-American students may view their academic abilities. The negative depiction of African-Americans in movies, television shows, news and advertising impact the perception African-American students have of themselves. The study will also explore how significant the role of the father is and potentially demonstrate to fathers how important a role they play in academic achievement and character development.

Limitations

This study focused on African-American students who are in their second years of college who are academically successful and placed in advanced placement courses with a grade point average of 3.0 or better and academically unsuccessful students who are in remedial classes because they have received a grade point average of 2.0 or less. This research is limited to African-

American students in a purposefully selected community college in New York State. It does not focus on the mother's influence on academic achievement.

CHAPTER 2: The Researchers Weigh In on the Family Structure

Introduction

Robert B. Hill explains in a 1972 study, "The strength of Black Families," how some African-American family structures, contrary to conventional wisdom, have provided the support for African-American students to succeed academically: "The achievement orientation of lower class Blacks attending college is very high, three out of every four coming from homes where the household head had no college education. Further, these students reported their parents expected them to graduate; White students surveyed on this question provided a much lower parental expectation." African-American students, however, had a higher regard to obtaining a college education than whites. In fact, though some would suggest a college-educated parent would support a college education more than a parent who did not, according to Hill's work African-American families proved that was not the case.

Wynona Bryant-Williams and Ronald Fannin in 1996 examined why a critical understanding of the African-American family is not examined and thus omitted entirely or treated peripherally. This was due in part to racism and prejudicial views that overshadow the positive contributions of the African-

American family, which leads to misconceptions and inaccurate presumptions related to its family structure. Bryant-Williams and Fannin explain, "The traditional perspective fails to focus on positive policies, programs, services, self-help efforts and coping strategies that are successful in strengthening the function of the African-American family." The needs of the African-American family structure do not differ from the needs and desires that other cultural families have in the United States. They have developed ways to strengthen and grow in a changing and evolving society. However, many of these positive developments have been overlooked or over-shadowed by prejudice and stigma. Robert B. Hill, Jaleel Abdul-Adil, and Alvin David Farmer Jr. in 2006 provided examples of positive development that are overshadowed by a negative perception of these characteristics that make up some African-American household: households headed by a woman or having other members of the family raise a sibling. **Parents have more frequent rates and diverse types of participation in their child's academic development than are commonly detected by or portrayed in mainstream research.**

Dorinda Carter identified in 2008 the skill set many African-American students utilize to achieve academically and she noted that an achievement ideology found in many students with high achievement incorporates a critical consciousness about race: that it has the potential to be a structural barrier constraining students' school and life success. This study examined how second-year community college African-American students with or without a father or a male surrogate successfully navigate in a predominantly white community college. In particular, what dimensions do they use when confronted by obstacles, and does the influence of having a father, male surrogate or neither a father or male surrogate influence the development of these dimensions. This chapter, then, is organized around the following six dimensions that high academic achieving African-American students use to navigate successfully in a racially hostile environment: critical race theory, personal identity, social sensitivity, racial identity, resilience, and a vision of success.

Critical Race Theory

Dorinda Carter in a 2008 study states, "Some black students maintain academic success by developing an acute understanding, that although racism might block their success, they will develop adaptive strategies for navigating this barrier in school." The way to understand this construct better is through a Critical Race Theory (CRT) framework. Richard Delgado and Jean Stefancic in a 2001 study explain, "Critical Race Theory began as a legal movement by activists and scholars interested in studying and transforming the relationship among race, racism, and power." Critical Race Theory, then, seeks to provide explanations for the experiences African-Americans have in social institutions, including education, for the purposes of eliminating social stratification through social justice.

The basic tenants of CRT, according to a 1995 Richard Delgado study, focus on:

1. Racism as normal in American society and strategies for exposing it in its various forms;

2. The significance of experiential knowledge and the use of storytelling to analyze the myths, presumptions, and perceived wisdoms that make up the common culture about race and that invariably render blacks and minorities one-down;

3. Challenges to traditional and dominant discourse and paradigms on race, gender, and class by showing how these social constructs intersect to affect people of color;

4. A commitment to social justice; and

5. An examination of race and racism across disciplinary fields.

Critical Race Theory furthers our understanding of how race and racism inform African-American students' achievement ideology and school behaviors, Daria Roithmayr concluded in "Introduction to Critical Race Theory in Educational Research and Praxis" in 1999. African-American high achieving students must develop an ideology that goes far beyond the limitation of the American achievement ideology, Dorinda Carter argued in 2008. African-American students must be able to develop their own ideas of what success is and not follow the American achievement ideology, which may prevent parameters that prevent an African-American student to believe that they can be successful. Carter explains the American achievement ideology: "It requires individuals to take ownership of their successes and failures, and it fails to account for structural conditions that might constrain or impede students' abilities to achieve." The negative stereotypes associated with African-Americans can lead to a student's fear of not being able to achieve one's goals. Carter explains the importance of having a high sense of positive racial identification combined with academic achievement counters this American achievement ideology.

Students who maintain high academic performance and a positive racial self-concept embody a critical race achievement ideology that allows them to both view themselves as achieving within the context of being African-American and overcome perceived racism in the school environment, Carter concludes.

Dr. Janie Victoria Ward in a 2000 study, "The Skin We're In," identified the relationship between CRT and the development of African-American high achieving students:

> Critical Race Theory reflects aspects of resistance in that it forms when African-American students internalize messages from family members and other adults in their lives that build a strong racial self-concept –resistance born from ... love and purpose, racial pride, and connection.

Critical Race Achievement Ideology originates in students' views of themselves as successful members of their racial group and their school successes as individual and collective racial group accomplishments, Dorinda Carter adds. Critical Race Theory states that African-American students who sustain their cultural background and are able to balance between their cultural setting and different setting are the most successful in achieving academic success. Some of these techniques students use are referred to as code switching and line straddling.

Line Straddling

When students utilize these adaptive and resistance-born concepts from Critical Race Theory, one of the coping mechanism that are born from this is Line Straddling. Line Straddlers bridge the gap between the cultural mainstreamers and the noncompliant believers. Carter in 2006 stated that a Line Stradler is a strategic navigator, ranging from students who "play the game" and embrace the cultural codes of both school and home community to those who vocally criticize the codes of both school ideology while still achieving well academically. In other words, a student who may come from the inner city and attend a school where he or she is a minority is able to embrace friends and cultural differences and succeed academically. Janie VictoriaWard confirms in a 2000 study, "The Skin We're In," that the most successful student is able to go back to his or her own community and maintain a cultural connection to his or her ethnic group.

Prudence L. Carter's 2006 findings in "Straddling Boundaries: Identity, Culture, and School" indicate that students who strike the best academic and social balance are those who are defined as "cultural straddlers." Straddlers understand the functions of both dominant and non-dominant cultural capital and value and embrace skills to participate in multiple cultural environments, including mainstream society, which consists of their school environments, as well as their respective ethnoracial communities:

> Students of color who believe education can be a vehicle for upward mobility, strive to do well in school by acquiring the cultural codes required for school success while also recognizing the value of

their own cultures, navigating effectively between their primary cultures and the dominant cultures.

A socially and academically successful student is one who can interact in both environments and understand the importance of both environments in his or her growth as a person and student.

Code Switching

One of the controversial factors Germine H. Awad in 2007 outlines as a reason for the lower level of academic achievement among African-American students is "oppositional identity," "acting white," and general anti-intellectualism. "Non-cognitive factors such as racial identity, academic self-concept, and self-esteem, have also been studied to identify the pertinent variables related to academic achievement," Germine H. Awad concludes. Awad introduces two phenomena in African-American culture not considered associated with academic success: "The burden of acting white, which contends that Black students become Race-Less to compete in academic domains." In some instances African-American students may feel the need to "act white" in order to be accepted in a predominantly white society or school. Though they are able to fit in with their white peers, they become rejected and ostracized by their African-American peers in their community.

The most frequent reference to "acting white", pertained to language and speech styles, Carter states. In Dorinda Carter's 2005 study, "In a Sea of White People: Analysis of the Experiences and Behaviors of High-achieving Black Students in a Predominantly White High School" by Harvard University Press, peers teased co-ethnic or same-race peers for how they spoke if they perceived the latter as emulating whites, rather than speaking black slang, a commonly shared vernacular style amongst urban minority youths. Carter concluded that approximately one in 10 of the students' evocations of the acting-white label dealt with their beliefs and perceptions of when the boundaries of ethnic solidarity were being transgressed, specifically when they felt that co-ethnics acted in ways that either disrespected or denigrated other members of their ethnic or racial group.

Some students believed that when co-ethnics or same-race peers touted their intelligence at the expense of another or put on "airs," then those students believed that they were better than other students. Carter explains that putting on "airs" or "acting white" had the same dynamics of racial dominance that these students encountered. If an African-American student is "acting-white," he or she has encompassed all the traditions and characteristics of white society. He or she has relinquished all or most of his or her African-American culture to date, which can include language, style of dress, music, and peer interaction. Code switching amongst African-American students focuses on the ability of that student to take on the necessary traits to fit successfully into that environment. By code switching the student has the ability to jockey between persona, thereby acquiring information that will allow him or her to navigate in that environment. The important difference that should be noted is code switching demonstrates that the individual temporarily adopts the predominant traits of the predominant environment for sustainability. Acting white infers that an African-American has given up his racial identity and values to acquire what he or she deems are the "better" identity. Their African-American peers perceive this change as "selling-out," which leads to ostracizing and rejection.

Critical Race Theory explores the ideas that African-American students' awareness of how their race is viewed by their peers and instructors affects the way they view their abilities to succeed in America. Charles G. Woodson's *The Miseducation of the Negro* explores how these negative perceptions make their way in the classroom and how these perceptions by instructors are perceived by their black students. In Woodson's 1933 work, he explains how blacks were miseducated in the American educational system and how it provided the atmosphere for blacks to believe that their race will not prosper. He explains that "to handicap a student by teaching him that his Black face is a curse and that his struggle to change his condition is hopeless is the worst sort of lynching." The reinforcement of negative depictions of African-Americans in history can produce an African-American student body with a lack of self-confidence that they can be successful academically or professionally. He explains, "He (teacher) teaches the Negro that he has no worth-while past, that his race has done nothing significant since the beginning of time, and there is no evidence that (blacks) will ever achieve anything great." Woodson's work aligns itself with Critical Race Theory; it demonstrates that students who are aware of how their race is negatively perceived by their peers or instructors can feel worthless and taught to accept failure as their only option. Woodson expresses that once African-Americans graduate they are almost taught to shed their heritage and to adopt the white man's culture, which would lead them to success as long as they stay in a "negroes place." He states, "When a Negro has finished his education in our schools, then he has been equipped to begin life of an Americanized or Europeanized White man." Consequently, this produces a view that leads to a lack of pride and disassociation of cultural identity amongst black students.

The attitude amongst blacks becomes that to be successful we must act white.

Personal Identity

John Ogbu and Signithia Fordham conducted a 1986 study about black students' success coping with the burden of acting white by identifying minority responses to discrimination in a school setting. They stated, "Two additional factors from the dynamics in minority communities also contributed to the school performance differences, collective identity and cultural frame of reference." Collective identity refers to people's sense of who they are. The persistence of a group's collective identity depends on the continuity of the historical and structural external forces that contributed to its formation. Collective identity develops because of one's experiences and is maintained by status problems and minority responses to status problems. These collectively help create and affect one's personal identity, these researchers conclude. One's positive self – identification or personal identity--is necessary to sustain school success. For such an identification to form and persist there must be the perception that one has the skills and resources to prosper, Claude M. Steele concluded in his book *A Threat in the Air: How Stereotypes Shape Intellectual Identity and Performance.* High achieving African-American students claim ownership for their performance and strive to use their personal strengths to improve their weaknesses, Carter argued in a 2008 study.

Ethnic identity includes attitudes and feelings toward a group of people believed to have a common ancestry, shared history, shared experiences, and shared cultural traits. Racial centrality is the extent to which race is considered to be a core part of one's identity, Cokley and Moore said in 2007.

Dorinda Carter's study identified a young African-American high achieving student's view on where she acquired her personal identity. Rachel, a senior believed that she was black and smart and emphasizes how her father instilled this belief in her:

> When I was little he used to, like, tell me all the time that I'm black and I'm different from people and for me, I dunno, just I have to work hard because you know white people don't think highly of black people, you know? Stuff like that…. It's kinda good cuz in a way I'm really, like, aware of the fact that I'm black…. My dad has taught me a lot about my background. So I still know about my history and what [sic] it is – what it actually means to be black. And I'm secure in my sense of self. I'm secure in my race and how smart I am.

Her father has racially socialized Rachel to the world around her, and being an achiever is a character trait embedded in her self-definition as a black person, Carter argues. The father introduces the idea that it is important to be successful academically and be able to take on the necessary traits to fit into that environment, but it is just as important to hold on to your cultural identity.

Racial Identity

William Cross, one of the scholars at the forefront of the racial identity movement, in *The Negro to Black Conversion Experience,* developed in 1971 the nigrescence, or the psychology of becoming black. He outlined five stages that blacks undergo in developing their identities: pre-encounter, encounter, immersion/emersion, internalization, and internalization-commitment.

Pre-encounter

The African-American has absorbed many of the beliefs and values of the dominant white culture, including the notion that "white is right" and "black is wrong." Though the internalization of negative black stereotypes may be outside conscious awareness, the individual seeks to assimilate and be accepted by whites, and actively or passively distances him/herself from other blacks.

Encounter

This stage is typically precipitated by an event or series of events that forces the individual to acknowledge the impact of racism in one's life. Faced with the reality of not being truly white, the individual is forced to focus on his or her identity as a member of a group targeted by racism.

Immersion/Emersion

This stage is characterized by the simultaneous desire to surround oneself with visible symbols of one's racial identity and an active avoidance of symbols of whiteness. As individuals enter the immersion stage, they actively seek out opportunities to explore aspects of their own history and culture with the support of peers from their own racial background. Typically, white-focused anger dissipates during this phase because so much of the person's energy is directed toward his or her own group and self-exploration. The result of this exploration is an emerging security in a newly defined and affirmed sense of self, William Cross argues. Cross introduced the immersion/emersion stage to demonstrate the difference between seeking out the characteristics of a culture to gain opportunities by taking on small parts of that culture in comparison to completely letting go your own cultural characteristics and adopting another culture to gain opportunities.

Internalization

While maintaining his or her connections with black peers, the internalized individual is willing to establish meaningful relationships with whites who acknowledge and are respectful of his or her self-definition. The individual is also ready to build coalitions with members of other oppressed groups.

Internalization-Commitment

The fifth stage is characterized by their "personal sense of Blackness into a plan of action or a general sense of commitment," William Cross states. African-American students focus more on the benefit of their academic success as a collective group or the contribution to African-American society than the benefit of academic achievement as individual success.

Germine H Awad in a 2007 study, "The Role of Racial Identity, Academic Self- Concept, and Self -Esteem in Predicting Academic Outcomes in African-American Students," identifies racial identity as a variable that may be related to African-American academic achievement. A child first identifies himself or herself with other children and at the heart, Awad explains, is the school. Students compare themselves to each other because they are able to view differences of one another. The school may provide the first meeting or interaction a student may have with a different ethnicity and how that meeting goes or is handled by the teachers may lead to inaccurate views and opinions and sweeping generalizations, as well as the development of inferiority complexes.

The American educational system does not provide a sound environment for African-American students to identify themselves positively. "The mis-education stage is the experience of being educated in the American School system, in which the focus is primarily on Western cultural history, and the significance of black history is not considered," Germine H.Awad states. The history taught from a Western cultural perspective fails to incorporate the rich and positive history of African-Americans. It highlights the struggles of slavery and oppression faced by them. African-American students who are engaged in learning in these environments may succumb to these negative images and feel that because of the history they will not be able to obtain a bright future.

To address issues that Awad identified, James A. Banks in 2006's "Culturally Diversity and Education: Foundations Curriculum and Teaching" introduced five phases of multicultural education that should be integrated into the United States educational system. These five phases introduce a narrow approach initially but slowly begins to broaden based on the spectrum of groups incorporated in a multicultural education model. In Phase I, Mono-ethnic Courses, African-Americans and other ethnic groups respond to their need and aspirations. The assumption was that only a member of an ethnic group should teach a course about that group. The majority of focus was based on white racism and how whites have oppressed African-Americans. It was believed that African-American studies were only needed by African-Americans.

Phase II, Multi-ethnic Studies Courses, is when white ethnic groups such as the Jewish and the Polish began to demand inclusion of their histories into curriculum of schools and colleges. These courses had become more global, conceptual, and scholarly. Banks explains, "They also became less political [sic] and began to explore diverse points of view and interpretations of their experience."

Phase III, Multi-ethnic Education, is the phase in which it was realized that even with the introduction of ethnic studies in schools it was not sufficient enough for real effective education reform. The negative attitudes of the teachers, combined with the academic results by minority students that were sub par when compared to their white counterparts, led many to believe that more needed to be done. James A. Banks states, "Research emerged that indicated how students of color are often placed in low academic tracks because of middle class and Anglo biased IQ exams." A more broad design for change would need to be developed in order to have a real impact. Educators begin to see that the school as a whole needed change, not just courses and curriculum.

In Phase IV, Multicultural Education, the sense of pride and racial identification that would take place with these or similar positive historical facts taught in the schools could lead to a progressive attitude for African-American students during their school experience, leading to better relationship development with teachers and peers. Banks explains,

> Multi-education became the preferred concept in many educational institutions ... the concept enabled schools, colleges, and universities to pool limited resources and to focus on a wide range of groups rather than limit their focus to racial and ethnic groups.

Phase V, Institutionalized Education, focuses on the process of implementing phases I through IV. Multicultural education enriches the society. It provides a way citizens can perceive and solve personal and public problems, Banks adds. The involvement in different ethnic cultures allows a student to become a part of the world and all the varieties of cultures and knowledge that is available.

Banks explains that the goals of multicultural education are to:

> acquaint each ethnic and culture group with the unique cultures of other ethnic groups...reduce the pain and discrimination the members of some ethnic and racial groups experience in their schools and in wider society because of their unique racial, physical, language and cultural characteristics.

As society has become more diverse, it is becoming increasingly important to understand the differences each group may have and the importance to educate everyone on each other's history. The ability to educate each other on cultural differences can lead to less stereotypes and inaccurate assumptions.

Social Sensitivity

To successfully earn academic achievement in an all-white educational setting, African-American students develop social sensitivities in order to move within and between various sub-cultures, and to understand the utility of acquiring the cultural capital of various cultural formations including those of success, Richard Delgado-Gaitan and Enrique Trueba concluded in their 1991 study. Alberto Carbera, Amary Nora, Patrick Terenzini, Ernest Pascarella, and Linda S. Hagedorn's 1999 study "Campus

Racial Climate and Adjustments of Students to College" examines the role that prejudice and discrimination play within the adjustment to college for African-American students. It hypothesizes that a student's pre-college academic ability has a direct influence on academic and intellectual development during the first year in college, and the decision to persist. Pre-college ability is posited as having a direct influence on the persistence of the student and exerting a stronger effect in African-Americans than any other non-minorities. The model developed in their study regards parental encouragement as facilitating the transition of the student to college. It exerts a positive influence on a student's education, aspirations, and his or her decision to persist in college. Because of this isolation in the classroom and in student-related activities, the African-American student is more likely to be deprived of the opportunity to learn new skills and concepts. African-American high achievers develop strategies for maintaining academic success by not viewing school success as white property. The successful student is cognizant of the social sensitivities that allow him or her to take full advantage of educational experience.

In Carla O'Connor 1997 study "Dispositions toward Collective Struggle and Educational Resilience in the Inner City: a Case Analysis of Six African-American High School Students" posited the idea that a student who works hard and always puts forth maximal effort in school can achieve academic success in school is associated with white middle-class students and not African-American students. This research, however, focused on six, low-income, African-American adolescents who were high achieving and expected to realize their ambitions while articulating an acute recognition of how race, class, and gender operated to constrain opportunity. O'Connor states, "Instead of identifying hard work, individual effort, and education as the primary determinants of how one makes it in the U.S., they (African-American students) recognize that the status attainment system operates to the disadvantage of people like themselves." In the classroom, a high achieving student will need to still hurdle the obstacle of racism; therefore, regardless of the grades they receive the fact that you are an African-American can stand alone from being a student.

Mendoza Denton, Rodolfo Downey, Valerie Davis, Geraldine Purdie, and Janina Pietrzak in a 2002 study "Sensitivity to Status-Based Rejection: Implications for African- American Students in College" found that preexisting anxious expectations of race-based rejection play a formative role in African-American college students' transitions to a predominantly white university. They discovered that this leads to a difference in the quality of inter-group relationships and goal realization. The findings resulted in race- based rejection expectations in the African-

Americans in the absence of explicit reference to race/ethnicity. African-American students would enter college with the idea that their race was perceived negative by their peers and teachers.

Expectations of race-based rejection were viewed as rooted in the high school experience or even prior educational experience and developed as an adaptive mechanism to cope with the possibility of being negatively targeted in the future. Many African-Americans college experiences can be based on how well they are able to develop social sensitivities.

Resilience

Resilience in the educational realm can be characterized as children's ability to achieve despite the risk factors such as poverty, single parent household, multiple siblings, and a young caregiver, according to a Bonnie Bernard study in 1991, "Fostering Resiliency in Kids: Protective Factors in Family, School, Community." A black student who has strong racial pride and heightened sensitivity to negative intellectual stereotypes about his or her racial group may take on a "prove-them-wrong" attitude in the classroom where those stereotypes exist, Dorinda Carter says. These students see their race as a strength that gives them the pride to accomplish. They have a great understanding of their heritage, not just the oppressive past but also the rich culture. They incorporate the positive history to surmount the racial obstacles.

Some African-American students may feel that they cannot compete academically. They quit in anticipation of not doing well. "When psychological disengagements occur in the domain of academic achievement, it is also known as academic disidentification," Kevin Cokley and Paula Moore say in "Moderating and Mediating Effects of Gender and Psychological Disengagements on Academic Achievement of African-American College Students." Motivation to learn is an important factor in academic achievement. When students begin to detach themselves from achievement they are at risk of dropping out of school. A clear understanding of the importance of academic self-concept may play an important role in the academic success of African-American students.

In Dorinda Carter's 2008 study, high achieving African-American students viewed achievement as a means to an end. Success is the attainment of a desired outcome related to an individual's quality of life, such as completing high school, entering college, or owning a business. The participants in Carter's study defined success as getting good grades, feeling good about themselves, having a strong social support network, and being goal oriented. Achievement indicates a student's accomplishment of specific tasks or goals. A student achieves success by an individual's ability to maintain acceptance by the social groups to which he or she desires to be apart; thus, school success is a holistic outcome of child development, Carter concludes.

Parental Awareness

Hill, Bryant-Williams, Fanin, and Carter have shown that parental involvement in schools increases the successful academic and behavioral performance of their children in schools. Abdul and Farmer suggest that parental involvement in schools is a national priority for both educators and researchers to promote the successful schooling of contemporary youth. The involved parents participated in multiple ways in their children's lives both inside and outside schools. Alberto Carbera, Amaury Nora, Patrick Terenzini, Ernest Pascarella, and Linda Hagedorn discuss in 1999's "Campus Racial Climate and the Adjustment" how parental influence factors into college students' transition into college. The model resulting from their study regards parental encouragement as facilitating the transition of the student to college; it exerts a positive influence on a student's education, aspirations and, as mentioned, on the decision to persist in college. The more a parent is engaged in the educational development of their children leads to higher achievement and can help overcome misconceptions about the educational experience.

Academic Self-Concept

Academic self-concept is an evaluative self-perception that is formed through experience with and interpretation of one's school environment, according to a 1976 study, "Self-Concept: Validation of Construct Interpretations" by Richard Shavelson, Judith Hubner, and George Stanton. It is possible to posit that academic self-concept influences educational attainment level, Herbert Marsh and Rhonda Craven noted in "Reciprocal Effects of Self-concept and Performance from a Multi-dimensional Perspective: Beyond Seductive Pleasure and Uni-dimensional" in 1997, and is influenced by socio-economic structure and family structure, M.D.R.Evans, Jonathan Kelley, and Richard Wanner said in "Educational Attainment of the Children of Divorce" in 2001. Beliefs about one's ability is a key construct in various motivational and self-concept theories, according to a 2004 study by Frederic Guay, Simon Larose, and Michael Boivin called "Academic Self-concept and Educational Attainment level: a Ten-year Longitudinal Study."

James P. Connell and James G. Wellborn's 1990 model of the self-system process proposed that when perceived competence (i.e., perceiving oneself as being effective in one's interaction with school activities) is fostered by the school context, engagement is likely to be manifested in affect, cognition, and behavior, which in turn lead to school outcomes such as grades, skills, adjustment, and persistence. A student's realization of competence within a school environment leads to obtaining academic success in many facets of school activities.

Frederic Guay, Simon Larose, and Michael Boivon's 2004 study tested the relation between academic self-concept and level of educational attainment. They hypothesized that academic achievement, socio-economic status, family structure, and academic self-concept would predict positively children's level of education attainment. The results suggest that among equally able students, those who perceived themselves as competent in school activities attain a high educational level in young adulthood.

James P. Connell and James G. Wellborn 1990's, and Frederic Guay, Simon Larose, and Michael Bovin's 2004 studies demonstrate that with a positive family structure that encourage a student's ability to succeed educationally leads to a student's engagement in school activities and academic success. A positive family structure implies the encouragement by parents to the student to involve themselves in extra-curricular activities in school that may involve interacting with students outside their ethnicity.

Vision of Success

The mainstream achievement ideology requires individuals to take ownership of their success and failures, but it fails to account for the structural conditions that might constrain or even impede students to achieve their maximum potentials in school and life, Carter argued in 2008. Success is defined as the achievement of a desired outcome related to an individual's quality of life, such as completing high school, entering college, or owning a business.

Na'ilah Nasir, Amina Jones, and Milbury Mclaughlin in their book *What Does It Mean to Be African-American? Construction of Race and Academic Identity in an Urban Public High School* in 2008 viewed two levels of context that bear on the youth's vision of achievement and success: the school and local context and the historical and national media context. The school and local context is important because different configurations of identities are possible through modeling, norms, and social interaction, according to a 2008 study by Na'ilah Nasir Amina Jones, and Milbury Mclaughlin. Nasir and Jones explain, "The historical and media context for African-American youth reinforces stereotypes of these groups as potentially dangerous, anti-intellectual, and downtrodden." Thus, prevalent stereotypes about African-American students and the ways those stereotypes are perceived by students may form an important part of the context that students negotiate, the researchers say.

Ellen Amatea, Sandra Smith-Adcock, and Elizabeth Villares in a 2006 book called *From Family Deficit to Family Strength* suggested that an individual's ability to prosper in the face of hardship is partly reliant on the individual but also on the support structures of that individual's own family and community networks. O'Connor in 1997 found that participants who did not possess strategies for overcoming constraints to their social and economic mobility did not have a positive vision of their own success because they did not have examples of black role models who overcame barriers to success in their own lives. The combination of a student's willingness to overcome obstacles and the family structure in place to guide and influence his or her navigation is equally important in achieving academic success.

Dr. Janice Victoria Ward in 2000 suggested that high racial centrality and positive racial regard is nurtured by a counter-narrative conveyed by parents who emphasize pride and self-respect as members of the racial group. These students' race-conscious parents are explicit in expressing the importance of high levels of achievement as a member of a sub-dominant racial group in America. Carter explains, "This view of success as an individual and collective group accomplishment helps students internalize success as a member of a racial group and maintain success and strong racial self-definition." Achieving academic success while maintaining cultural identity and awareness is as important as academic achievement, and this is nurtured by the parents.

Naïve Theory

Annette Taylor and Patricia Kowalski's "Naïve Psychological Science: the Prevalence" 2004 research centers on the how naïve science arises from faulty conclusions based on limited personal experience and observations, social interactions, and inaccurate prior instruction. This results in a learning schedule that is resistant to change. Ninety introductory students took a pre-test and questionnaire based on relatively recent misconceptions. They also took a post-test and described why they believed the item was a misconception and where they got the information. The students were shown that once they realize the source of their misconceptions they were able to learn not to take everything they read, see on television, and hear from a friend as a credible source; thus, they targeted students' conventional wisdom about concepts.

"Science education literature suggest that so called 'Naïve Science' arises from faulty conclusions based on limited personal experiences and observations, social interactions, and inaccurate prior instructions," Taylor and Kowalski noted in 2004. Change in an educational institution that seeks to accept and understand the African-American culture will not take place instantly and because of certain factors is prohibited. This can lead to a widening of the gap between the African-American community and educational system. Taylor and Kowalski's study shows that strongly held, but incorrect beliefs, are particularly difficult to change. They state, "Once misinformation becomes fixed in a person's knowledge base, new information is frequently distorted or ignored, resulting in strengthening or retention of the inaccurate belief."

Views and beliefs that may have a negative reflection on an ethnic group may be difficult to change if there is not awareness of the importance to create change that will be sustainable. "The conceptual change literature provides extensive evidence that strongly held beliefs are especially too difficult to change," these researchers concluded. They explain that much of the literature on misconceptions have focused on behavior rather than the process of change. Taylor and Kowalski provided literature that helps understand what is needed to negate negative views and misconceptions about African-American family structures, aptitude, and community. Their research shows that massive change is unlikely to occur and a more stage-orientated change method approach must take place that will transfer knowledge from one stage to the next and will enable growth and change from misconceptions to a conceptual understanding about the African- American student, community, and family.

Summary

African-Americans are attending college more than ever. According to Hill, Bryant-Williams and Fannin, the family structure is arguably the key reason for this incline. Overshadowed are the positive policies, services, and community support that helped in the success and strength of the family. Dorinda Carter's 2008 study focused on nine high achieving African-American students in a predominantly white high school. The research determined that students developed adaptive techniques to succeed in a racially hostile environment. However, her study did not apply the parental contribution to the development of those dimensions. The dimensions drawn from her research and other studies examined have enabled the development of six dimensions that support the idea that community and family structures may determine academic achievement for African-American students.

The first dimension is Critical Race Theory, which provides an understanding of how African- Americans attitudes and understanding of their resilience and abilities assist them in being successful in a predominantly white environment. They also develop mechanisms that allow them to acquire educational capital and still maintain cultural identity.

The second dimension is Personal Identity, which is how one sees him or herself is a key factor in academic success. William E. Cross' *The Negro to Black Conversion*

Experience in 1971 developed the stages of nigrescence and outlines five stages that African-Americans undergo to develop their identity.

The third dimension, Social Sensitivity, addresses the ability of African-American students to move in and out various subcultures. Having the awareness of who you are and how your race is perceived and adapting to the environment to obtain a positive outcome enables you to acquire your goals without losing your own identity.

The fourth dimension, Resilience, provides the core trait African-Americans have used through the beginning of the slave trade to present day to succeed despite the odds. Encountering obstacles and learning to adapt despite racial hostility is one of the attributes Carter discusses in 2008 as a coping mechanism used by successful African-American students.

The fifth dimension of Academic Self-Concept is a way African-American students view their abilities compared to their peers. James P. Connell and James G. Wellborn in 1990 demonstrated that with a supportive family structure it increases the achievement of the African-American student.

The sixth dimension, Vision of Own Success, is the achievement of a desired outcome. Carla O'Connor's "Dispositions Toward (Collective) Struggle and Educational Resilience in Inner City: a Case Analysis of Six African-American High School Students" in 1997 explained that the individuals possess adaptive strategies that overcome social and economic restraints have a positive vision of their own success. Ellen Amatea, Sandra Smith-Adcock and Elizabeth Villares in 2006 identified the individual's family and community networks as a pivotal contributor to developing one's vision of success.

The six dimensions are cultivated and developed by a strong family and community foundation. Dorinda Carter provides a 2008 study that identifies that high achieving African-American students' utilization of Critical Race Theory to navigate through a predominantly white educational environment successfully. The parental involvement is considered by researchers Hill, Aschenberger, Bryant-Williams, and Fanin as not prevalent in the rearing and educational development of children; in fact, much of the focus is put on what the students adopt or had to overcome. In many instances, the support of the community and family provides the tools that these students utilize to achieve academically and socially.

The influence the family structure had and the importance of maintaining the cultural identity was a continuous theme in each dimension presented. The absence of a parental guide in achieving success can lead to fear of interacting socially with other ethnicities and limiting the goals a student may set for themselves. The development of pursuing goals that are not under the American ideology of success can prevent African-American students from feeling that their goals are not relevant and not attainable.

CHAPTER 3: The Sample of Students Studied

Introduction

The purpose of my study was to investigate how African-American students with or without a father or male surrogate presence at home develop their personal identity, academic self-concept, their own race theory, social sensitivities, resiliency, and a vision for their own success. The study sought to examine whether or not there was a relationship between academically unsuccessful and successful African-American students who have a father present, a father not present, or a male surrogate influence their success in a community college environment. Since the African-American family continues to be the preeminent mechanism for socialization and for pooling resources for upward mobility, it was essential that the fathers should be viewed as peripheral, thereby making sure not only that the perceived weaknesses were examined, but that the perceived strengths were as well.

Setting

The study included African-American students enrolled in a community college located in New York. The college has 10,000 undergraduate students and currently enrolls approximately 3,200 African- American students, of which 1,920 are black women and 1,280 black men. 5,760 white students, 2,080 Hispanic students, 1,082 Asian or Pacific Islander, and 12 American Indian or Alaska native make up the remaining student body.

Selection of Participants

The participants in this study were college students who had completed two years of community college, and enrolled in advance placement and remedial classes. An informant identified student respondents designated as academically successful or unsuccessful African-American student who have either a male surrogate, or a father, or neither a father nor male surrogate in their lives. The criteria for the participants were given to the informant who then provided college personnel with the criteria needed for each student to meet to be included in the research. The personnel selected the students who met the criteria and supplied the list of students for the research. The students were sent a letter of invitation to become a part of the research. A total of 16 students were selected, consisting of nine males and seven females. The participants were as follows: Of the nine male respondents there were six academically successful males (two with a father, two with a male surrogate, two without a father or a male surrogate) and three academically unsuccessful male students (one with a father, one with a male surrogate, one without a father or a male Surrogate). Of the seven female respondents there were three academically successful females (one with a father, one with a male surrogate, one without a father or a male surrogate) and four academically unsuccessful female students (two with a father, one with a male surrogate, one without a father or a male surrogate). (See table 3.1)

Table 3.1 Second Year Status

Father status	Successful male	Successful female	Unsuccessful male	Unsuccessful female
Father in Home	2	1	1	2
Male Surrogate in Home (available)	2	1	1	1
None	2	1	1	1

Data Gathering Techniques

Permission to conduct the study was obtained from Dowling College in New York and the Community College Institutional Review Boards (IRB) for the Protection of Human Subjects in Research. After obtaining IRB approval and prior to the interviewing procedure, potential participants were contacted initially by mail, then via telephone to explain the study and determine their interest in participation. Prior to the interviews, the principal investigator reviewed and collected the consent forms. At the start of each meeting, a student was presented a description statement describing the purpose of the study. The data for this study was collected using semi-structured, open-ended interviews. The interviews took place at the college or other participant-designated location, at a time determined by the participant and the principal investigator. The interview process took approximately 60 minutes to complete. There were 26 questions and required follow-up questions that were asked during each interview.

Data were reported in the participant's own words based on audiotape recordings and field notes. Transcriptions of interviews and setting descriptions collected were the primary source for analyzing the data. All data gathered remained in the personal possession of the researcher and kept in a locked safe in the researcher's personal office. Pseudonyms were used to identify participants in audio responses.

All the audiotapes of interviews were destroyed upon the completion of the transcription process. Any documentation that had the name of the participants was destroyed to protect the participant's confidentiality.

Interview Protocol

After a review of the research literature, a semi-structured interview protocol was developed around the following themes: critical race theory, as defined by Richard Delgado and Jean Stefancic's *Critical Race Theory: an Introduction* in 2001; social sensitivity, as noted by Concha Delgado-Gaitan and Henry Trueba's *Crossing Cultural Borders: Education for Immigrant Families in America* in 1991; resiliency, according to Bonne Bernard's *Fostering Resiliency in Kids: Protective Factors in the Family, School, and Community* in 1991; academic self-concept, as stated by Germine Awad's *The Role of Racial identity, Academic Self-concept, and Self-esteem in the Prediction of Academic Outcomes for African-American Students* in 2007; and vision of own success, following Dorinda Carter's "Achievement as Resistance: the Development of a Critical Race Achievement Ideology among Black Achievers" in the *Harvard Educational Review* in 2008.

Data Analysis

The research questions that guided this study focused on academically successful and unsuccessful African-American students who are second-year students in a community college with or without a father or male surrogate presence as it relates to the following dimensions: critical race theory, social sensitivity, resiliency, academic self-concept, and vision of own success. The data were organized around emergent themes and patterns; once organized, the data were examined for the emergence of themes, patterns, and discrepancies.

Question One

How do academically successful and unsuccessful African-American sons and daughters who have second-year status in a community college with or without a father or male surrogate present describe their personal identity?

Data were analyzed based on emergent themes, patterns, and discrepancies.

Question Two

How do academically successful and unsuccessful African-American sons and daughters who have second-year status in a community college with or without a father or male surrogate present describe their academic self-concept?

Data were analyzed based on emergent themes, patterns, and discrepancies.

Question Three

How do academically successful and unsuccessful African-American sons and daughters who have second-year status in a community college with or without a father or male surrogate present describe their own race theory?

Data were analyzed based on emergent themes, patterns, and discrepancies.

Question Four

How do academically successful and unsuccessful African-American sons and daughters who have second-year status in a community college with or without a father or male surrogate present describe their social sensitivity?

Data were analyzed based on emergent themes, patterns, and discrepancies.

Question Five

How do academically successful and unsuccessful African-American sons and daughters who have second-year status in a community college with or without a father or male surrogate present describe their resiliency?

Data were analyzed based on emergent themes, patterns, and discrepancies.

Question Six

How do academically successful and unsuccessful African-American sons and daughters who have second-year status in a community college with or without a father or male surrogate present describe their vision of success?

Data were analyzed based on emergent themes, patterns, and discrepancies.

CHAPTER 4: The Present Study's Family Structure Findings

Introduction

This study examined whether or not there is a relationship between academically successful and unsuccessful African-American students with or without a father or male surrogate present, and the influence of their presence on their academic success in a community college environment. A semi-structured interview protocol was developed around the following themes: critical race theory, social sensitivity, resiliency, academic self-concept, and vision of own success. Sixteen African-American second-year community college students were interviewed; their comments were examined for the emergence of themes, patterns, and discrepancies.

The research questions, as already listed in Chapter 3, guided the study:

Question One

How do academically successful and unsuccessful African-American sons and daughters who have second-year status in a community college with or without a father or male surrogate present describe their personal identity?

Question Two

How do academically successful and unsuccessful African-American sons and daughters who have second-year status in a community college with or without a father or male surrogate present describe their academic self-concept?

Question Three

How do academically successful and unsuccessful African-American sons and daughters who have second-year status in a community college with or without a father or male surrogate present describe their own race theory?

Question Four

How do academically successful and unsuccessful African-American sons and daughters who have second-year status in a community college with or without a father or male surrogate present describe their social sensitivity?

Question Five

How do academically successful and unsuccessful African-American sons and daughters who have second-year status in a community college with or without a father or male surrogate present describe their resiliency?

Question Six

How do academically successful and unsuccessful African-American sons and daughters who have second-year status in a community college with or without a father or male surrogate present describe their vision of success?

Description of Participants

Once again, as already noted in other sections of this book, the participants were 16 African-American second-year college students who attended a diverse community college in New York; nine were males and seven were females. The students were grouped by their academic level and whether or not there was a presence of a father or male surrogate. For the purpose of this study, academic successful and unsuccessful were defined as follows: a student enrolled full time in his or her second year of college, having a grade point average of 3.0 or better, and who had obtained 30 credits or more and were currently enrolled in an advanced placement program and considered academically successful. An academically unsuccessful community college student is defined as a student enrolled full time in their second year of college, having a grade point average of 2.0 or who had obtained less than 30 credits, and were currently registered in a remedial program.

There were nine males: two males who were academically successful with a father in their home; two males who were academically successful with a male surrogate in their life; two males who were academically successful without a father or male surrogate; one male who was academically unsuccessful with a father in his home; one male who was academically unsuccessful with a male surrogate in his life; and one male who was academically unsuccessful without a father or male surrogate in his life. The seven females consisted of one female who was academically successful with a father in her home; one female who was academically successful with a male surrogate in her life; one female who was academically successful without a father or male surrogate; two females who were academically unsuccessful with a father; one female who was academically unsuccessful with a male surrogate; and one female who was academically unsuccessful without a father or male surrogate.

KF1 was a male academically successful student whose father died when he was younger and his older brother became his male surrogate.

EB3 was an academically successful female student who has both her parents in the home.

RF12 was a male academically successful student whose father died when he was 7 years old. He has no father or male surrogate. He prides himself on his Caribbean culture that enables his family to support one another so well.

JB13 was a female academically successful student who does not have a father or male surrogate.

PG4 was a male academically successful student whose parents divorced but his father is involved in his life.

AY8 was a male academically successful student whose father is present but does not influence him.

NB9 was a female academically successful student who has had contact with her father for the last few years but looks to her grandfather as a male surrogate.

DC10 was a male academically successful student who recently met his father for the first time. He was raised by his surrogates: five uncles and his grandfather.

D16 was a male academically successful student whose father is currently incarcerated and has been since he was 4 years old. He has no male surrogate.

JJ2 was a male academically unsuccessful student who grew up in a household of women and did not have a relationship with his father.

ER5 was a male academically unsuccessful student whose cousin has stepped into the role as male surrogate.

VH6 was a male academically unsuccessful student whose father takes an active role in his life.

CH7 was a female academically unsuccessful student whose father is present in the home and has influenced her greatly.

VR11 was a female academically unsuccessful student who looks to her brother as her male surrogate. She gives him the title of "Papi," a term of endearment for the level of respect she has for him.

MC14 was a female academically unsuccessful student whose father is in the home but she views him as having no role in her life.

RA15 was a female academically unsuccessful student whose father has been recently released from jail and was trying to establish a relationship. Prior to that she has had no father or male surrogate in her life.

Table 4.1 identifies the gender, academic success or unsuccessfulness of the students reported by the student, with or without a father, or male surrogate present in the home.

Table 4.1 Participants

Participant	Gender	Academically Successful/Unsuccessful	Father/Male Surrogate/None
KF1	Male	Successful	Surrogate -- Brother
EB3	Female	Successful	Father
PG4	Male	Successful	Father
AY8	Male	Successful	Father
NB9	Female	Successful	Surrogate -- Grandfather
DC10	Male	Successful	Surrogate – Uncles and Grandfather
RF12	Male	Successful	None
JB13	Female	Successful	None
D16	Male	Successful	None
JJ2	Male	Unsuccessful	None
ER5	Male	Unsuccessful	Surrogate -- Cousin
VH6	Male	Unsuccessful	Father
VR11	Female	Unsuccessful	Surrogate -- Brother
MC14	Female	Unsuccessful	Father
RA15	Female	Unsuccessful	None

Question One

Research question one allowed academically successful and unsuccessful African-American sons and daughters who have second-year status in a community college with or without a father or male surrogate present in the home to describe their personal identity. Successful African-American students describe the development of their personal identity as a combination of not being concerned with the perception others had about them and not comparing themselves to others academically, a positive view of self, drive that pushes them to prove others wrong, and seeing the value of adaptation. The themes that emerged from the academically successful African-American students were: 1) race-less, 2) view of self, 3) drive, 4) adaptation, and 5) cultural identification. These themes are defined as: 1) race-less, which is the ability to interact with others without identifying their race as a reason to interact or not interact; 2) view of self, which is one's perception of him or herself; 3) drive, which is the willingness and determination one has to accomplish their goals; 4) adaptation, which is the ability to interact with a culture not your own and balance between entering your culture and another without giving up your cultural identity; and 5) cultural identification, which is a student's ability to identify their heritage.

The pattern that emerged for the race-less theme is academically successful male and female students with or without a father or male surrogate in the home choose friends based on what they have in common and not race. The pattern that emerged from view of self theme were academically successful male and female students with a father in the home have a high level of confidence in their academic abilities, which they use to identify themselves. The pattern that emerged from the drive theme were academically successful male and female students with a father or male surrogate in the home were focused on personal gain, eagerness to be successful, and to prove wrong the negative stereotypes that certain media outlets portray and instructors have of African-Americans. The particular stereotypes by the media are of images of African-Americans involved in crimes, dropouts from educational institutions, and possessing no drive educationally. The particular stereotypes by instructors are that African-American students are not concerned with achieving academically at a high level. The pattern that emerged from adaptation was the benefit academically successful males and females with a father in the home or a male surrogate, and without a father or male surrogate in the home, felt were received from interacting with other ethnic groups. The pattern that emerged from cultural identification were academically successful male and female students with a father in the home or a male surrogate, or without a father or male surrogate, identifying their heritage and family support in the pursuit of high academic achievement.

Race-less

Academically successful

Academically successful male and female students with or without a father or male surrogate in the home demonstrated that they choose friends based on what they have in common and not ethnicity. Though there are cliques on campus, they suggest that these cliques are created to prevent other ethnic groups from entering into their groups. However, very few have peers that belong to ethnic-group cliques. Academically successful male and female African-American students see that as a way of limiting their ability to learn about new things.

JB13 spoke about her relationship with other students outside her ethnicity: "I have a lot of different friends in different ethnic groups. I have Muslim friends. I have white friends, Asian friends, we're all cool." D16 explains the value of having a positive attitude about interacting with students outside his ethnicity and how a negative attitude leads to misconception:

> Well, the way I describe it, it closes opportunities for them because I feel that people that are willing to share necessary info with them are less likely to

do it because of the attitude that is perceived when they're looked at in some way.

RF12 explains:

> Diversity is basically a huge component of the school; it's part of the school's identity, a person like me coming from the inner city, it's almost like a culture shock in the sense that you have to step out of your comfort zone in order to make the right decisions or the moves that's going to advance you in terms of your college career.

Academically successful students view interaction with other ethnicities as a valuable tool that opens up opportunities to learn new things and have new experiences.

Research question one allowed academically successful and unsuccessful African-American sons and daughters who have second-year status in a community college with or without a father or male surrogate present in the home to describe their personal identity. Unsuccessful African-American students describe the development of their personal identity as a combination of developing relationships with people outside their ethnicities based on common interest, a low self-confidence, an inability to adapt to unfamiliar environments predominated by other ethnicities, and they view their ethnicity as a negative factor in pursuing success academically or socially. The themes that emerged from the unsuccessful African- American students were: 1) race-less, 2) view of self, 3) adaptation, and 4) cultural identification. Race-less is defined as the ability to interact with others without identifying their race as a reason to interact or not interact. View of self is defined as how one perceives themselves. Adaption is defined as the ability to interact with a culture not your own and balance between entering your culture and another without giving up your cultural identity. Cultural identification is defined as how a student identifies their heritage to themselves and others.

The pattern that emerged from race-less was that academically unsuccessful male and female students with a father in the home or male surrogate chose friends outside their ethnicity based on same interest (i.e., fashion and music). The pattern that emerged from view of self were that academically unsuccessful male without a father in the home or male surrogate demonstrate a lack of confidence in their ability to compete academically with other students and the negative perception portrayed by the media and some instructors also contributed to creating a low confidence in their academic ability. The pattern that emerged from adaptation of academically unsuccessful male students with a father in the home was that they view only relationships with others in their ethnicity as important and comfortable; this prevents many underachieving African-

American students from exploring relationships with other ethnic groups. The pattern that emerged from cultural identification was that academically unsuccessful male students with a male surrogate felt that due to the negative depiction of African-Americans in the media and negative perception by some instructors in the classroom there is a hesitation to demonstrate cultural pride. Consequently, an inferiority complex develops and prevents interaction with other ethnic groups.

Academically unsuccessful students did not indicate that those with a father or male surrogate, or without a father or male surrogate, influenced their drive.

Academically unsuccessful

Academically unsuccessful male and female students with a father in the home or male surrogate were open to developing new relationships with students outside their ethnicity but did not do it to gain academic capital, which is the reason academically successful students did. The students develop relationships based on recreational commonalities. VH6 states,

> I just go on what I have in common with the person. Like, you don't have to be black if you like rap music. If you like the same music that I like, then we have something to talk about and TV shows and everything else.

MC14 states,

> I wind up being friends with people of different cultures, so I really don't have a problem. A lot of people probably would wonder, oh, why she hang out with this color or this person like Pakistan, white, whatever, but for me I'm very open-minded to whatever.

View of Self

Academically successful

The academically successful male and female with a father or male surrogate in the home exhibited a high level of confidence in their academic abilities, which they used to define themselves. PG4 states, "I don't want to boast but I'm smart, but I wouldn't say I'm no genius, above average." Successful students walk into a classroom ignorant of any negative judgments and focused on doing the best they can academically. PG4 explains,

> Personally I have gotten the experience where I've stepped into a class and I could be the only black kid or one of the few black kids and let's say it's predominantly white or it's predominantly Asian, it's like whoa, what's this kid doing here.... That doesn't distract me in any way. That makes me want to do better.

Academically successful male and females without a father or male surrogate also exhibit a high level of confidence. D16, explains,

> I got lucky because in high school as I was graduating I got an internship at Bloomberg in Manhattan, and so as I was interning there as a PC technician all my co-workers were giving me a real big sense of confidence, and as I left I became a way more confident person.

Academically successful students use outside motivation to contribute to developing their confidence in their abilities to compete academically.

Academically unsuccessful

Academically unsuccessful males without a father in the home or male surrogate had low self-confidence and demonstrated more anxiety because of the absence of a father. JJ2 states:

> Growing up from birth to 13 years old, all the influences in my life were women. I grew in a house as the only boy, nine women …. If something happened my aunts would help me, whereas I felt that if I had a male influence It would be like let him pick it up on his own, let him be a man, let him carry his bike. Women will always mold, nurture, and I felt that always had an effect on my life.

JJ2 goes on to explain: "I'm a little bit more sensitive. I'm not really assertive as a male. I get along with women greatly and that [is] the advantage I got from that. I'm a good listener." The lack of relationship with a father or male surrogate gave JJ2 a complex about his ability to be a "man." He admittedly yearns for that relationship between him and his father that would help him obtain confidence. Academically unsuccessful students without a father or male surrogate define their view of self based on their outer appearance and popularity amongst their peers. MC14 states, "They look at me like maybe I'm a little crazy, outspoken, maybe a little freak or whatever they want to call it. Basically, it's people describing me because it's true." MC14 discusses how peers have influenced her academic shortcomings: "I could've really done what I had to do, because me being really too so-so, I let people really get into my head more than do what I have to."

Drive

Academically successful

Academically successful male and female students with a father or male surrogate in the home have inner drive that focuses more on their personal gain and eagerness to want to be successful and to prove "them wrong." The idea of proving "them wrong" stems from the negative portrayal placed on African-Americans by the media and negative stigmas associated with African-American students' ability to succeed academically by their teachers. PG4 explains how negative criticism by the media impacts him, saying it is, "fuel for me. That doesn't distract me in any way. That makes me want to do better."

EB3 explains how the media's negative perception effects him: "That makes me want to go harder even more."

KF1 explains,

> I know that everybody is doing the same thing and I don't want to be down there where everybody is up here talking about trying to understand this. I want to understand it more and interpret it in another way where I could help it towards my goals and my field.

The pursuit to be the best is constantly on the minds of academically successful students. In their pursuit of academic excellence, academically successful students demonstrate a competitive nature that will not allow them to settle for second best. PG4 says, "I've had to override some things that were very easy. Some things were harder than they seemed, of course. I've gone to tutoring. I've stayed extra hours. I'm not the type to just quit on it or just give up."

NB9 explains that academically successful students are very aware of the effect peers may have on their academics and show a strong innate sense of drive that propels them to overcome any peer pressure:

> Just not letting outside influences influence you on the inside and that's what I learned that whatever happens on the outside like that's OK, I need to

make sure I'm still peaceful and this may be a temporary struggle but in the long run I can just look back and it's not a big deal.

The effect on students dealing with peer pressure has been regarded as one of the hurdles they are confronted with today. When academically successful students are faced with academic hurdles there is nothing that stops them from obtaining the necessary tools to overcome their obstacles.

JB13 explains,

> Yeah, because when I was growing up I'd always see the same faces sitting on the stoop outside and I was just like, I can't be like that. I can't be the girl always sitting on the step for the next 10 years, so it kind of pushed me to be like you're gonna do this, you have to do this even if you don't want to, you have to.

Images of peers in the community that have underachieved gives academically successful students the drive to pursue academic excellence.

Adaptation

Academically successful

Academically successful males and females with or without a father or male surrogate in the home see the academic benefit more so than academically unsuccessful students. They are familiar with adapting to school norms, because they have members of their family who have benefited from adapting to school norms and have explained the benefit.

KF1 explains how his brother adapted to his work environment in order to be accepted:

> Yes, but it depends, in certain areas of my life, like when I used to do different things it used to trigger them off to where it was like is this person really is this person, why is he doing this? But then I changed my way of acting when I started to play off who they say I am.... Like my brother is a health administrator and the way he worked his way up to the top was going through extensive training, learning how to adapt himself to school faster and get himself up there on a higher level because they probably looked down at him the same way they did us. For him to go up higher without paying attention to other people, it showed that we could do the same thing. He gave me and my brother that example.

A key area of adaptation for academic successful students is acquiring academic advantages afforded to them by adaptation with other ethnic groups. NB9 explains:

> Well, it's good because I could deal with so many different people. If I have a bias I understand that I have a bias and I'm aware of other people's biases and how they have those biases, so I can work with

so many different people, which is great because sometimes black students they don't know how to do, like they're not in my same classes, so do I need to go to like the Chinese, Japanese, so it's like I know how to move around and be able to relate to each one.

A second key area is academically successful students with a father at home or a male surrogate, or neither a father nor male surrogate, use white peoples images of success as a benchmark of success. D16 explains how academically successful students are aware of the bias against African-American students and present an image that enables them to blend in and conform to his predominantly white educational institution. He states,

> Well, I don't really feel as if it (being in a predominantly white institution) had an academic effect on my being right now. In the face of higher-ups I feel like I'm not actually being myself, but I know that I can do whatever it takes necessary to create an image. Well, I feel that if I presented the image that I normally am at home people would probably look at me differently in terms of professionalism, work ethic, and things of that nature.

Academically unsuccessful

Academically unsuccessful male students with a father or male surrogate in the home are more sensitive about developing a relationship with other ethnicities because of there own insecurities to step out of their ethnic comfort zone and meet new people from different ethnic groups. Therefore, a pattern of displacing their feeling on the other ethnic groups appears. CH7 states, "It affects you because there are certain groups and certain cultures that you could even tell would prefer to be around their own people, in their own clique or their own group, because they feel more comfortable there." His assumption that students who are from other ethnic groups would prefer to interact with their own ethnic group rather than meet people outside of them demonstrates CH7 fear to adapt.

Cultural Identification

Academically successful

Academically successful male and female students with a father in the home or male surrogate, or without a father or male surrogate, find strength in identifying themselves as African-American. There is a sense of pride and accomplishment of being a few out of the many that are contributing to countering the negative perception instructors, whites, and news outlets associate with African-Americans academic abilities. Society and media have put images of African-Americans as looking a particular way. One area has been in skin color. Many of the roles in television and movies are given to lighter skin African-Americans. This can also be said for many of the commercial, print ads, and advertisements involving African-Americans. This can be very discouraging for African-Americans who do not fit the image of what society and media considers acceptable and attractive. KF1 sates, "I'm a dark-skinned African-American who is very determined." KF1 describes how his dark-skinned complexion can be seen as a negative attribute by news outlets and movies. He is conscious of the views society places on the complexion and the relationship between his skin color and his African ancestry. He views his skin complexion not as a distraction or hindrance in the journey to academic success.

Many of the participants believe that the election of our country's first black president gave African-American children aspiration to set out to do whatever they dream possible and accomplish it. JB13 explains,

> Like when Obama became president every African-American person that I knew thought they could do whatever they wanted in the world. It's like a confidence booster, that's some person who looks like me and look where they are, maybe I could make it there, too.

President Barack Obama changed the landscape for African-American students, making what was thought of as unrealistic to achievable through hard work and dedication regardless of socioeconomic background.

Academically unsuccessful

Academically unsuccessful male students with a male surrogate view their cultural identification as an African-American negatively. There is a sense that they have no control over how that view is looked at in the present or how they can change it in the future. ER5 confers,

> If I had to say, like honestly I'd probably say they see me as African- American. Because when it comes down to it, like if there's a problem they realize that you are an African-American and an African-American don't make it through school like that.

Discrepancy

Academically unsuccessful female students did not indicate the influence of a father or a male surrogate or neither a father nor male surrogate have on their personal identity.

Question Two

Research question two allowed academically successful and unsuccessful African-American sons and daughters who have second-year status in a community college with or without a father or male surrogate to describe their academic self-concept. Successful African-American students describe the development of their academic self-concept as a combination of how they viewed themselves, identifying their heritage as a source of strength, and showing strength through adversity. The themes that emerged from the successful African-American students were: 1) view of self, which is how one perceives him or herself; 2) cultural identification is how students' express their heritage; and 3) resilience, which is the ability to persevere despite encountering obstacles.

The pattern that emerged from the view of self theme was that academically successful male and females students with a father in the home developed a high level of confidence in their academic abilities. The pattern that emerged from cultural identification theme was that academically successful male and female students with a father in the home or male surrogate or without a father or male surrogate define themselves as African-American. They may have been from Caribbean descent; however, they identify themselves as African-American. The pattern that emerged from the resilience theme was that academically successful male students with a father in the home or a male surrogate had the ability to succeed despite hardships.

Research question two allowed academically successful and unsuccessful African-American sons and daughters who have second-year status in a community college with or without a father or male surrogate present in the home to describe their academic self-concept. Academically unsuccessful students without a father or male surrogate develop their academic self-concept through interaction with peers.

Academically unsuccessful students develop their academic self-concept through interaction with peers or parental influence. JJ2 explains, "Peers push me to do more. I like to feel good about myself when I speak to other races especially about myself… and I feel good about myself when I'm teaching them something." Academically unsuccessful students with a father or male surrogate develop their academic self-concept from their parental influence. It becomes what they use to guide them in understanding the potential they have academically. ER5 states, "They always say that I can do better. They already see it in me. They always know I can do better." He continues to explain about his relationship with his (cousin) male surrogate: "He definitely pushed me. When I say pushed me, ya know, stuff that I didn't think I could do, he would push me."

View of Self

Academically successful

Academically successful male and females students with a father in the home used their academic success to define who they were or had a general self-concept. They enjoyed walking into a classroom and demonstrating their superior abilities despite an instructor's or peer's negative perception about their ethnicity.

PG4 states,

> The first thing my daddy loves telling me is you already got a strike against your name, as a matter of fact two strikes against your name, because you're a black boy, so you have to work twice as hard in your life to get what you need or what you want. And that's just breaking the barrier, he's not even talking about going above and beyond to make what you want as a success.

PG4 was raised to acknowledge the view that whites and news outlets have placed on African- American students. In many instances, he suggests that you cannot be surprised by the banner you wear when you walk into a classroom. Though it maybe negative you must be focused on who you are and who you want to be.

Academically successful students take the view their parents want for them but also extract the view they want for themselves based on their academic experiences. D16 explains,

> Through the words of my parents I always thought that in order to be successful I'd have to really make millions of dollars, and things of that nature. But then as I came to school and I noticed the true value of education, the union between different

subjects, I noticed that success is actually what makes you most happy.

Cultural Identification

Academically successful

Academically successful male and female students with a father in the home or a male surrogate, or without a father or male surrogate, identified themselves as African= American. However, they used their Caribbean heritage as inspiration to overcome academic obstacles.

EB3 explains her cultural influence on her academic achievement:

> A young African-American...my family's influence on me? Hmmm, I mean they kinda have high expectations for me and everything because my family is like Caribbean, so not most of them went to college, so I'm basically like the first generation to go to college.

Though they identify themselves as African-American, academically successful students find their cultural heritage as a backbone to pride, structure, and strength. PG4 states,

> Well, I got a Caribbean family. Everybody knows knowledge is everything, without it...a real Marcus Garvey quote is, "People without knowledge is like a tree without roots." It's fundamental in my

household. Before first and everything you gotta have school, you gotta have a background, you gotta have some kind of education and know where you're coming from and know where you'll be later on.

Resilience

Academically successful

Academically successful students with a father in the home or a male surrogate demonstrated a strong sense of resiliency defined in their ability to overcome discrimination because of their success in school and placing a strong emphasis on showing that they can succeed in the face of adversity in the classroom.

The influence of peers on a student's success can be great at times. KF1 explains,

> Like when I said I was determined and dedicated, I used to say that to people, but what I was actually doing, I was actually a follower in a sort of way where I used to follow other people and get sucked into peer pressure. But now as I grow and get more knowledge and get more wisdom I learned how to fully grasp the fact that I am a determined and dedicated African-American. I can help myself. I don't need anybody help…. I'll give you an example, like if you're going to school and you know you want to get that "A," there's somebody always talking about others or "Let's go out and have fun a little bit" and then we come back to that

"A," but we might not have that much time to get that "A," so to me as a person I'm thinking, "I want 'A,' so I rather do with that 'A' than to play around and get myself in trouble by getting a 'B.'"

The academically successful student's resilience is fueled by obtaining academic success.

Question Three

Research question three allowed academically successful and unsuccessful African-American sons and daughters who have second-year status in a community college with or without a father or male surrogate to describe their own race theory. Academically successful African-American students describe the development of their own race theory as a combination of understanding how certain instructors may view them and how their culture contributes to their views about race. The themes that emerged from the successful African-American students were: 1) perception of instructors and 2) cultural identification. Perception of instructors is defined as how an African-American student perceives how a professor views his or her ethnicity and how the professor demonstrates his negative or positive view of the student's ethnicity to the student directly or in front of his or her peers. Cultural identification is defined as how a student identifies his or her heritage to themselves and others.

The pattern that emerged from the perception of instructors theme was that academically successful male and female students with a father in the home or male surrogate viewed the negative perception teachers had of them not as a distraction and did not distract them from wanting to do well in that class. In many instances, it fueled their ambition to do well. The pattern that emerged from the cultural identification theme was that academic successful male and female students with a father in the home had strong feelings of pride in their heritage when it comes to succeeding academically.

Perception of Instructors

Academically successful

The way an instructor may view a student's ability can affect a student in two ways: it can either push them to do well, or hamper their abilities and cause disinterest in the subject matter. Academically successful male and female students with a father in the home or male surrogate used an instructor's negative view of them as motivation.

> JB13 states,
>
> Sometimes I think that race is perceived, like they'll see a black student...like I have friends who are African-American and they'll wear their pants down and do-rags and stuff like that and then teachers will not look at them as not knowing

much, but then when they start talking about stuff they know, it's like I wouldn't have expected that to come out of your mouths....I've had classes where I have had Caucasian teachers that would definitely treat me different from a Caucasian student...I'll give you an example. There was a time, because I used to take college courses in high school, so when I got here and I took my first English course it was the same thing that I did in high school, so I would sometimes be real lackadaisical in class and stuff like that and one time I did fall sleep and the teacher bugged at me to wake up and then there was another student who was Caucasian and she was like "Oh, sweetheart, you gotta get up" and I was just like...seriously? Really? So I felt some type of way about that.

The academically successful student is aware that teachers give a different preference to certain students and do not allow that to discourage them from being successful in the classroom.

In some instances, teachers verbally mention their criticism of African-American students in front of a full classroom. D16 states,

> Well, some teachers try to discourage you because of my race from the start saying some of these students...there's a good certain number of you, probably a small percentage of you are going to pass and the rest of you are going to fail. They try to discourage you and in my eyes I just look at that as wrong.

D16 is aware of how his race may be viewed by his instructors but does not allow that to determine how he feels about his academic abilities or how he views his race.

Academically successful male and female students view a teacher's negative perception of them as affirmation that they must work harder and that they are held to a different set of standards than other students in the classroom. They use this perception by the teacher as one way to fuel their academic success.

Research question three allowed academically successful and unsuccessful African-American sons and daughters who have second-year status in a community college with or without a father or male surrogate present in the home to describe their own race theory. Academically unsuccessful African-American students describe the development of their own race theory based on the negative perception their instructors had about their ethnicity's ability to do well academically. The theme that emerged from academically unsuccessful African-American students with a father at home or a male surrogate was: 1) perception of instructors. Perception of instructors is defined as how an African-American student's perception of how a professor views his or her ethnicity and how the professor demonstrates his negative or positive view of the student's ethnicity to the student directly or in front of his or her peers.

The pattern that emerged from the perception of instructors theme was that academically unsuccessful students with a father or male surrogate at home were hesitant to contribute in class and interact with other students outside their ethnicity. In the opinion of academically unsuccessful African-American students, the negative views by the instructors were also recognized by other students in their classroom and in some cases this view was adopted by them. It could be argued that the instructor's perception could have contributed to other students' existing perception of African-American students or created a new perception. Subsequently, this leads to apprehension and social isolation resulting in ideological segregation.

Academically unsuccessful

Academically unsuccessful male students with a father at home or a male surrogate allowed instructors perceptions that African-American students cannot succeed academically affect the way they interacted in the classroom, as well as how they did academically in the classroom.

The perception that a teacher has of a student is not only viewed by the student but by his or her classmates as well. ER5 states,

> Some teachers, I have had some teachers that were like "Yo." Like they be like I've never seen someone as intelligent as you being an African-American I wouldn't…so I'm like what are African-Americans, dumb? I don't take it as anything. I try not to let anything bother me.

Academically unsuccessful students were affected academically by the perception the teacher had of him or her. They didn't have the foundation to combat negative racist ridicule by their teacher that could lead to overcoming the negative perception. VH6 states,

> I would say my 7th grade teacher because I had a problem with something and he kind [of] just didn't listen. Not only kids are cruel sometimes but that's expected, but coming from a teacher it really hurts because I failed two of his tests straight and I did as well as I could and did not know what it was, and I kept asking him what I'm doing wrong and he shrugged it off and when I failed all the tests he started cracking on me in front of the class and said, "Well, since you ain't gonna be nobody, this is what you're going to be and yes, man, you're going to be in your 30s with a T-shirt or a hat on saying, 'I am stupid,' now hit me for 25 cents" and that's how successful you're going to be all because I didn't know a math problem and also because I

struggled with my reading and he kind of saw that as being funny, but it wasn't funny, it was a serious threat on my half.

Cultural Identification

Academically successful

Academic successful male and female students with a father in the home use cultural identification when defining where they developed their understanding of the importance of education. Carter's 2008 study demonstrates the importance of the combination of strong cultural pride and academic achievement that leads to challenging the mainstream achievement ideology. African-American students are sometimes left out because of the negative racially pathologies associated with being African-American The value of education and the instrument that it becomes to navigate through the American educational system is reiterated by family matriarchs who tend to be from Caribbean descent. EB3 said, "I mean, they kinda have high expectations for me and everything because my family is like Caribbean." PG4 said, "Well, I got a Caribbean family…. It's fundamental in my household. Before first and everything, you gotta have school."

Discrepancies

Academically unsuccessful students did not indicate the influence of their father or male surrogate, or neither a father nor male surrogate, had on their cultural identification.

Question Four

Research question four allowed academically successful and unsuccessful African-American sons and daughters who have second-year status in a community college with or without a father or male surrogate to describe their social sensitivities. Successful African-American students describe the development of their social sensitivities as an opportunity to learn from a number of different ethnic groups and demonstrate that friendships can transcend ethnicity. The theme that emerged from the successful African-American students was adaptation. The pattern that emerged from the adaptation theme was that academically successful male and female students with a male surrogate and without a male surrogate or father at home seek to build relationships with other ethnic groups and see this as a way to enhance their academic experience.

Adaptation

Academically successful

Through the exchange of different ideas from different cultures, academically successful male and female students with a male surrogate and without a male surrogate or father at home view this as a way to develop new friendships, new ideas, and more importantly a way to learn from others academically.

NB9 states that she,

> Can work with so many different people, which is great because sometimes black students, they don't know how to do, like they're not in my same classes, so do I need to go to like Chinese, Japanese, so it's like I know how to move around and be able to relate to each one.

The view that the world is bigger than your community is adapted by academically successful students. They envision themselves as world leaders and see the benefit of learning about other ethnicities now, so they can prepare for their future. D16 explains, "It closes opportunities for them because I feel that people that are willing to share necessary info."

Research question four allowed academically successful and unsuccessful African-American sons and daughters who have second-year status in a community college with or without a father or male surrogate present in the home to describe their social sensitivity. Academically unsuccessful African- American students describe the development of their social sensitivities by expressing their resistance to exploring relationships with students outside their ethnicity because of their fear of rejection and because of their academic shortcomings. The theme that emerged from academically unsuccessful African-American students was adaptation. Adaption is defined as the ability to interact with a culture not your own and balance between entering your culture and another without giving up your cultural identity. The pattern that emerged from the adaptation theme showed academically unsuccessful students without a male surrogate or father in the home demonstrate unfamiliarity with developing relationships outside their ethnicity. They don't have family members or access to people in their life that can show them the benefit of learning and socializing outside their ethnicity. Consequently, they develop limited knowledge of other ethnicities and may develop their own negative perception about other ethnicities.

VR11, a unsuccessful student with a male surrogate states,

For me, I feel more comfortable, just certain things I can't say around certain people, they won't understand as a (non-minority) person.... Everybody comes together in a way as far as minorities. But the white folks or whatever, they stick together, but us blacks and Latinos, yeah, we stick together.

Academically unsuccessful

Academically unsuccessful students with a father at home and without a male surrogate or father in the home are not willing to engage with other ethnicities because of their insecurities of not being able to compete academically. JJ2 explains, "More the way I speak, I guess I feel a little intimidated with other races."

Academically unsuccessful students are not willing to take the first step to develop a relationship with other ethnicities. They allow their limited knowledge of that ethnic group to decide the benefit of getting to know that ethnicity. CH7 says,

> It [not knowing a lot about of other ethnic groups] affects you because there are certain groups and certain cultures that you could even tell would prefer to be around their own people, in their own clique or their own group because they feel more comfortable there.

Question Five

Research question five allowed academically successful and unsuccessful African-American sons and daughters who have second-year status in a community college with or without a father or male surrogate to describe their resiliency. Successful

African-American students describe the development of their resiliency as a combination of overcoming a negative perception an instructor may have of the student, showing that the negative depiction of African-American students by the media does not apply to them, and overcoming personal hurdles that they would not allow to distract them from succeeding academically. The themes that emerged from the successful African-American students were: 1) instructor's perception, which is the negative preconceived view a professor may have about a student; 2) media, which is defined as television shows, news outlet, movies, and newspapers and the effect it has on African-American students perception of themselves; and 3) resiliency, which is the ability to persevere despite encountering obstacles. The pattern that emerged from the instructor's perception theme was that academically successful students with a male surrogate, despite some professor's negative view of them or negative verbal comments made about African- Americans, did not allow those factors to distract them from succeeding in the classroom. In many instances, it was ignored or used as inspiration to do well. The pattern that emerged from the media theme was that with academically successful male and female students with a male surrogate or without a male surrogate or father there is an obvious understanding of the negative portrayals of African-Americans in the media. However, these portrayals are used as inspiration to change that negative depiction. The pattern that emerged from the resiliency theme was that academically successful students with a father in the home place a strong emphasis on showing that they can succeed in the face of adversity in the classroom.

Instructor's Perception

Academically successful

Academically successful students with a male surrogate see the negative perception of African-Americans by their instructors as damaging to the normal psyche of a student. However, because of their acknowledgment that this is the society that they live in, they prepare themselves mentally and in many instances surround themselves with individuals who have the same ideology and same ambition. KF1 states,

> They view us as people who don't stress to be the top. They feel like we're gonna always be average or a little below average…. There's a whole bunch of people, which is good, that's African-American on campus….like now it's starting to be more of a common thing with a lot of people now. Not to say that they still don't degrade us or they still don't think of us as somebody that's high [achieving].

Academically unsuccessful

Academically unsuccessful students with or without a father or male surrogate demonstrated resiliency in overcoming non-academic circumstances. A15 explains, "When I first came here I didn't speak English at all, so people made fun of me or whatever. Sometimes I have problems with words, but I ask and then just learn."

VH6, an academically unsuccessful student with a father, states, "I just kept telling myself you can't fail because all my friends are off to college and doing their thing and I haven't spoken to them in a long time, and I want to be on own their same level."

Media

Academically successful

Academically successful male and female students with a male surrogate and without a male surrogate or father are aware of the negative depiction of African- Americans in the media but do not allow that to define who they are or who they are going to be. In fact, they use it as inspiration to be successful. NB9 states,

> I've learned to reject the media…. Just like how you have to be the best at what you do and then like my grandfather, too, he's like you have to be the best in the class against all these people, you have

to be No. 1. So, you have to strive for excellence, you don't want to be normal, you have to stand out.

The negative portrayal by the media of African-Americans leads to a feeling of frustration. JB13 states, "I think that it is because of ethnicity sometimes because when you see the negative life of being non-successful it's usually African-American people." However, academically successful students are able to see the media for what it truly is.

Academically unsuccessful

Academically unsuccessful male and female students with a father or male surrogate allow the media to determine their definition of success VH6 explains,

> Basically, what I saw in the media is that if I want to be successful there's one of two things, either you know how to rhyme or you could be an athlete. But the media did not show me, my family showed me that you could get more than that stuff. Like all these guys who make money beyond the scenes, the agents, the lawyers, and stuff.

The media contributes to the pressure academically unsuccessful students face when defining what success can be for them. VR11 confers,

You could say, in a sense, yes and no because coming from a point like this, hmm, how can I put this? Not that I'm basically going with the media, but I learn from that, how to move certain things, what to do or not to do or basically thinking outside the box rather than in the box, going against the norm.... You sit in front of the television and basically you learn a lot from there and it dumbs you down really. It depends on what you watch, all that you watch, everything. Anything will take a toll on you, especially students now. We have the whole issue of beauty or they paint, they make you feel like the only way you can be successful is if you're a lawyer or a doctor or something like that. You have certain shows [where we are criminal and uneducated] and all the stuff like that. Yeah, so all that mixed together it can take a toll on people.

Unsuccessful academic students derive their knowledge of success, beauty, and the view of themselves by what the media depicts.

Resiliency

Academically successful

Academically successful male students with a father in the home are mindful of the stereotypes media outlets and stereotypes by white professors has placed on them and are conscious of the uphill battle and welcome the obstacles. PG4 says,

> Well, there's a standard within everybody's culture and everybody's race and I guess in one sense or another I'm black. You look at the average black kid and it's like, you know what, he's probably not going to get out of high school. I know this, I recognize this. And if he is in college, well, what's to say he won't drop out and pretty much sling crack rock or do basketball or whatever sports have you.

Academically successful students want to play an integral part in making a difference in the negative opinions in society. They acknowledge the views but do not allow the views to hinder their academic success.

Research question five allowed academically successful and unsuccessful Africa-American sons and daughters who have second-year status in a community college with or without a father or male surrogate to describe their resiliency. Unsuccessful African-American students describe the development of their resiliency as living up to the standards that the media has provided for defining a successful African-American. Media's standards suggest that if you cannot obtain a certain degree or certain career you are considered not successful. For some academically unsuccessful students they give up on academics because these career goals endorsed by the media differ from what they feel are realistic goals for themselves. The theme that emerged from the unsuccessful African-American students was media--defined as television shows, news outlet, movies, and newspapers--and the effect it has on the perception an African-American student has about their ethnicity

The pattern that emerged from the media theme was that academically unsuccessful students with a father and male surrogate allowed media's influence to limit their aspirations academically and socially. The negative depiction of African-Americans affected the way unsuccessful academic students would view themselves compared to other students. In some instances, unsuccessful students would fear that they were associated with the negative depiction of African-Americans in the media and would not try to socialize outside their ethnicity because they feared rejection. ER5 explains, "When it comes down to it, like if there's a problem, they realize that you are an African- American and African-Americans don't make it through school." JJ2 anticipates rejection: "My hair, my identity, when they see the whole Rastafarian thing. Other races may think I am doing nothing with my life. They may not think I am as bright as the rest."

Discrepancies

Academically successful male students indicated the influence that their father or male surrogate had on how they view their instructor's perception about them and how their father or male surrogate influences the development of their resiliency. Academically unsuccessful male students did not indicate the influence of their father or male surrogate, or the lack thereof, on their resilience and instructors' perception.

Question Six

Research question six allowed academically successful and unsuccessful African-American students who have second-year status in a community college with or without a father or male surrogate to describe their vision of success. Successful African-American students describe the development of their vision of success as a combination of the high level of discipline that male surrogates and fathers enforced to ensure that their sons or daughters would work hard and live up to their full ability; a high level of confidence exhibited by the student in their academic abilities that they use to overcome their fears and obstacles, searching for recognition for their accomplishments from peers, media, and instructors; and competing with a father who is not present in the home or in the student's life.

The themes that emerged from the successful African-American students were: 1) disciplinarian; 2) future orientation; 3) validation; and 4) ghost father. Disciplinarian is defined as a father or male surrogate enforcing strict guidelines to ensure high academic achievement that must be followed. Future orientation is defined as how African-American students view their chances of achieving their goals. Validation is defined as the acknowledgment of one's academic ability by instructors, media, and ethnic groups outside their own. Ghost father is defined as an African-American student who does not have a father present in his or her life but continues to compete against the father in an "I am going to show him" attitude. Despite never meeting their father, his absence is still felt. The pattern that emerged from the disciplinarian theme was that academically successful students with a male surrogate or father present in the home were given a high level of discipline by their male surrogates and fathers. The pattern that emerged from the future orientation theme was that academic successful male students with a father in the home create the vision they see for themselves from their interaction or advice from their male surrogate or father. His input lays the foundation for their ideas and leads to their own ideology of what their vision of themselves will incorporate. The pattern that emerges from the validation theme was that academically successful male and female students with a father in the home or male surrogate felt validated when they demonstrated their academic abilities equaled or surpassed their ethnic counterparts. The pattern that emerged from the ghost father theme was that academically successful and unsuccessful males without a father or male surrogate would compete with a father who is not present. They want to show the father who is absent that they are better than they are and the fact that he wasn't present in their life did not affect them.

Disciplinarian

Academically successful

The discipline demonstrated by their father or male surrogates propelled academically successful male students to do well academically. In many instances, the discipline imbedded a sense of support. KF1 sates,

> Yes, they beat us to the point that you had to do that. My brothers were like, we're not playing no games, you can't come home and not say we finished our homework.... He had more of an aggressive effect.... He [the brother] went over the homework if we didn't understand it, but you were supposed to understand it. That would be a way of saying that if you understand it, now you're gonna get it if you don't get it now. After I teach you how to do it, you better get it.

The father or male surrogate demonstrates the importance to achieve academically. The discipline given is a way of showing the importance and seriousness of academic achievement. The brother's goal is to embed in the mind of his younger brother that the only obstacle that prevents you from achieving your goals is that you and hard work are necessary.

Academically unsuccessful

Academically unsuccessful male and female students with a father in the home demonstrate a high level of discipline and disappointment when they cannot live up to the discipline their father has placed on them. CH7 states, "My father's influence, obviously he's a hard-ass. He's very, very tough on me, it's a little annoying, but I also feel bad when I don't succeed."

The acknowledgment of the father's strong discipline at home was not confused by the academically unsuccessful student as mistreatment. Rather, it is perceived that their fathers wanted to see them reach their true potential. VH6 talks about his dad's influence: "My dad was a good influence, he was[a] hard guy, but he ain't take any mess."

Future Orientation

Academically successful

Academic successful male students with a father in the home created the vision of their own success. They did not allow the negative depiction by news outlets and negative perceptions by professors prevent them from having goals that far surpassed what might be expected of them. PG4 explains, "You step into the box and you make it yours. You look at reality and you try to make your own imagination with it [what your future can be]."

Academically unsuccessful

Unsuccessful female students with a father in the home developed their ideas of success by imitating what path their father or male surrogate chose. CH7 explains,

> He's the man because he worked somewhere for a lot of years and then they laid him off and he realized that he wasted a lot of time. He was unhappy with his job. He would've rather have been doing music and now he's doing music.... He's still not working, but he seems so much happier even without a job. Even though he's still worried about money, he's more relaxed because he wants to do his music; he's so focused on it. Even though he hasn't gotten to where he's gotten yet, he's finally finding some type of success because he's enjoying himself.

Some academically unsuccessful students find success in many non-academic areas. CH7 states, "I find success as finding out the thing that you really like or love and doing it no matter what anybody tells you."

Their parents may see that their talents may not be in academics. However, they instill in them that whatever they chose to do, do it well, but above all do what makes them happy.

Validation

Academically successful

Academically successful male and female students with a father in the home or male surrogate are often validated by their fathers or male surrogates based on their academic accomplishments. They want to be recognized for their academic achievements and like to be recognized for their academic abilities by white academically successful students. PG4 states,

> So, when I get a compliment from somebody outside my race that deemed supposedly to be doing better financially or academically than I am, it's a [motivator] to do more and it makes me stand on high because I could do better than you.

NB9 received validation from her own ethnicity, which made her proud that she was contributing to destroying the negative perception of African-American students. She explains,

> [I] think [that] all of it impacts me, but I feel like with black people it's like they really care, like they really care. When I was in Illinois they were like, I really appreciate what you're doing; it's nice to see black people [and I'm like], wow, that's interesting. Whereas people outside my race it's more like it's expected that you do well, where with black people it's different.

Academically successful students take the validation from their own ethnicity as a counter to negative images of African-Americans. In a sense, it becomes an affirmation that they are destroying the stereotypes and the community is acknowledging that. Academically unsuccessful students with a father or male surrogate look to their parents for validation. ER5 explains, "I want to see my parents proud of me."

Ghost Father

Academically successful

Academically successful male students without a father or male surrogate present in the home use the absence of a father or male surrogate as an inspiration to succeed and to make sure they do not end up ultimately repeating the cycle when they are fathers. D16 explains,

> Well, my dad is currently incarcerated. He's been incarcerated since I was in the fourth grade.... He was a chemistry teacher, so it wasn't like he just

went to jail and it was over for him, like the usual black male who gets incarcerated.

They subconsciously compete against the father and use that competitive fire to succeed. What is equally important is that though his father is not present, his father's presence is felt by his focus and determination to succeed academically. D16 states further,

> I go visit him a few times a year and he tries to help me with classes, gives me advice on what to do and he'd always have plans for me to do extra things, so I'm really grateful to my father for that.

C10 uses his father's absence and memories of him to drive himself. Though his father has not been in his life, there in his subconscious lives the ghost of a father that pushes him. He states,

> From what I did know about him growing up, I just knew that I didn't want to do the stuff he did. So, all I knew is that he graduated high school, so I did. He graduated high school, so I gotta one up him, so I graduated college. So, I just recently got my degree here.

Academically unsuccessful

Academically unsuccessful male students who have a male surrogate and do not have a father present in the home blamed their absent father for character flaws that they developed because of the absence of a male in their life. JJ2 sates,

> I think that if I had, he'd teach me how to be more of a provider. Because of the absence of that in my life this is what I want to be, a provider. And if I'm not a provider, then I can't be a provider. I try not to put myself in that situation…. But I do want to be a father; I just don't want to have a kid go through the same things that I went through.

The fear of passing on the same character flaws to his unborn children is evident in JJ2's willingness to want to learn to be a provider, which he feels he could only have learned from his father. The surrogates in his life were women, who he felt made him too sensitive and not assertive. He states, " If something happened, my aunts would help me, whereas I felt if I had a male influence it would be let him pick it up on his own, let him be a man." However, his surrogates did provide him with understanding the importance of an education. He states, "With personal experiences with failure in my life, being told that if you didn't go to school you're not going to be anybody."

The lack of a disciplinarian in his life is explained by ER5:

> I guess that if my dad was around I'd probably be more serious because without him being there I don't know where I developed it from but it just came out, I just develop this funny character, so if

anything I'm always in the light. I don't just get upset. I try to lighten it up.

ER5 demonstrates the need of structure that he feels could have benefited him in developing focus on his academics. Because of the lack of a father figure he feels that it prevents him from taking his coursework seriously.

Research question six allowed academically successful and unsuccessful African-American students who have second-year status in a community college with or without a father or male surrogate to describe their vision of success. Unsuccessful African-American students describe their vision of success as a combination of trying to live up to parental expectation, finding happiness in non-academic pursuits, overcoming character flaws they developed because of the absence of a male in their life. The themes that emerged from academically unsuccessful African-American students were: 1) disciplinarian; 2) future orientation; and 3) ghost father. Disciplinarian is defined as a father or male surrogate enforcing strict guidelines to ensure high academic achievement that must be followed. Future orientation is defined as how African-American students view their chances of achieving their goals. Ghost father is defined as an African-American student who does not have a father present in his or her life but continues to compete against the father in an "I am going to show him" attitude. Despite never meeting their father his absence is still felt.

The pattern that emerged from the disciplinarian theme was that academically unsuccessful male and female students with a father in the home recognized that strong discipline is used by their parents to produce the best effort academically from the students. When they did not receive discipline, it was perceived as a lack of concern with what academic path they chose. The pattern that emerged from the future orientation theme was that unsuccessful female students with a father in the home follow in the steps of their father or male surrogate and acknowledged that they may not be successful academically. However, it is important to choose a career path that makes you happy. The pattern that emerged from the ghost father theme was that academically unsuccessful male students who have a male surrogate and do not have a father or male surrogate expressed a lack of assertiveness and focus, and this has contributed to their poor academics and social skills.

Discrepancies

Academically unsuccessful females with a father indicated the fathers' influence on future orientation. Academically successful females describe their future orientation as having the ability to help other people reach their goals and influence others.

Academically successful males with a father describe their future orientation as working hard to get what you need and want.

Table 4.2 illustrates how each dimension has themes, patterns, and discrepancies that were analyzed using the data gathered from the participant responses above.

Table 4.2 Dimensions, Themes, Patterns, and Discrepancies

Dimensions	Themes	Patterns	Discrepancies
Personal Identity	Race-less	Academically successful and unsuccessful students were similarly influenced by race-less. They both developed friendships with students outside their ethnicity. This was influenced by both father or male surrogate.	Academically unsuccessful female students did not indicate the influence of a father or male surrogate
	View of Self	Academically successful student's personal identity was influenced by their father or male surrogate.	
	Drive		Academically unsuccessful students did not indicate that their father or male surrogate influenced their drive.
	Adaption		
	Cultural Identity		
Academic Self-Concept	View of Self	Academically successful students' academic self-concept was influenced by their father or male surrogate	Academically unsuccessful student's academic self-concept did not indicate father or male surrogate influence.
	Cultural Identity		
	Resilience		

Dimensions	Themes	Patterns	Discrepancies
Own Race Theory	Perception of Instructors	Academically successful and unsuccessful students with a father or male surrogate's perception of instructors indicated similar influence. Both indicated the negative perception of their instructors were due to negative stereotypes of their race and not their academic ability. The influences for both were from father or male surrogates.	
	Cultural Identity		Academically unsuccessful students did not indicate cultural identification
Social Sensitivity	Adaptation	Academically successful and unsuccessful students indicated influence by their father or male surrogate. Academically successful and unsuccessful students without a father or male surrogate present demonstrated the ability to adapt.	

Dimensions	Themes	Patterns	Discrepancies
Resilience	Perception of Instructors	Academically unsuccessful students did not indicate the influence their father or male surrogate had on their perception of instructors or resilience.	Academically unsuccessful males did not indicate the influence that their father or male surrogate had on their perception of instructors and resilience.
	Resilience	Academically successful females did not indicate influence on instructors perception and resilience	Academically successful male students indicated the influence that their father or male surrogate had on their instructor's perception and resilience.
	Media	Academically successful and unsuccessful students were influenced similarly by the media.	
Vision of Success	Future orientation	Academically successful males and academically unsuccessful females with a father present indicated the influence their father had on their future orientation	Academically successful females did not indicate the influence a father or male surrogate had on their future orientation. Academically unsuccessful males did not indicate the influence a father or male surrogate had on their future orientation.
	Validation	Academically unsuccessful students did not indicate the influence on their validation.	
	Disciplinarian	Academically successful and unsuccessful students indicated the same discipline a father or male surrogate had as disciplinarians.	
	Ghost father	Academically successful and unsuccessful males indicated the same influence not having a father or male surrogate had on a ghost father. Academically successful and unsuccessful females did not indicate a ghost father.	

Themes that emerged across the dimensions were view of self, cultural identity, adaptation, and resilience. View of self is defined as how one perceives oneself. Cultural identification is defined as how a student identifies his or her heritage to themselves and others. Adaption is defined as the ability to interact with a culture not your own and balance between entering your culture and another without giving up your cultural identity. Resilience is defined as the ability to persevere despite encountering obstacles. Academically successful students' views of self were influenced by their father or male surrogate in the dimensions of personal identity and academic self-concept. Students' cultural identity emerged in personal identity and academic self-concept. Adaptation emerged in personal identity and social sensitivity. Resilience emerged in academic self-concept and resilience. Academically successful students with a father or male surrogate present influenced the way academically successful students view their academic abilities.

Table 4.3 Patterns Emerging across Dimensions

Father or Male Surrogate	Male and Female	Successful Academically
View of self / personal identity	View of self / personal identity	View of self / personal identity
View of self / academic self-concept	View of self / academic self-concept	View of self / academic self-concept
Cultural identity / personal identity	Cultural identity / personal identity	Cultural identity / personal identity
Cultural Identity / academic self-concept	Cultural Identity/ academic self-concept	Cultural Identity / academic self-concept
Adaptation / personal identity	Adaptation / personal identity	Adaptation / personal identity
Adaptation / social sensitivity	Adaptation / social sensitivity	Adaptation / social sensitivity
Resilience / academic self-concept	Resilience / academic self-concept	Resilience / academic self-concept
Resilience / resilience	Resilience / resilience	Resilience / resilience

CHAPTER 5: Study Conclusions and Recommendations

Introduction

The purpose of this study was to investigate how African-American students who have a father presence at home, who have a male surrogate available, and who do not have a father or male surrogate presence at home develop their personal identity, academic self-concept, their own race theory, social sensitivities, resiliency, and a vision for their own success. The study sought to examine whether or not there is a relationship between academically successful and unsuccessful African-American students with or without the presence of a father or male surrogate and whether or not a male surrogate influences the students' success in a community college environment.

Summary

To address the purpose of the study, a semi-structured interview protocol was developed around the following themes: critical race theory, social sensitivity, resiliency, academic self-concept, and vision of own success, as referenced by aforementioned researchers. Sixteen African-American second-year community college students were interviewed. This chapter presents a summary, conclusion, and recommendations originated from the analysis of the data collected from the interviews of academically successful and academically unsuccessful African-American students and an analysis of the relevant literature.

Six research questions were responded to using the data obtained from the interviews with the students. Research question one asked academically successful and unsuccessful African-American students to describe their personal identity.

Research question two asked academically successful and unsuccessful African-American students to describe their academic self-concept. Research question three asked academically successful and unsuccessful African-American-students to describe their own race theory. Research question four asked academically successful and unsuccessful African-American students to describe their social sensitivity. Research question five asked academically successful and unsuccessful African-American students to describe their resiliency. Research question six asked academically successful and unsuccessful African- American students to describe their vision of success.

Sixteen students were selected: Of the nine male respondents, there were six academically successful males (two with a father, two with a male surrogate, two without a father or a male surrogate) and three academically unsuccessful male students (one with a father, one with a male surrogate, one without a father or a male surrogate). Of the seven female respondents there were three academically successful females (one with a father, one with a male surrogate, one without a father or a male surrogate) and four academically unsuccessful female students (two with a father, one with a male surrogate, one without a father or a male surrogate). Academically successful community college students who were enrolled full time in their second year of college had a grade point average of 3.0 or better, and had obtained 30 credits or more and were enrolled in an Advanced Placement program. Academically unsuccessful community college student were enrolled full time in their second year of college, had a grade point average of 2.0 or obtained less than 30 credits, and were registered in a remedial program.

The father or male surrogates role in the development of an academically successful African- American student goes beyond the academic achievement in the classroom. There is a passing of negative and positive experiences that shape the human nature and academic abilities the father or male surrogate shares with the student. These experiences may deal with how their ethnicity may or may not have been an obstacle interacting with other ethnic groups and academic success. Academically unsuccessful students without a father or male surrogate struggled with adapting to a predominantly white environment and developing relationships with ethnic groups outside of their ethnic group.

Academically unsuccessful African-American female students with a father or male surrogate exhibited that they measure success based on their abilities to make choices that influences their quality of life. Although they may not have high academic achievement, they developed a high level of independence and strong character from their father or male surrogate. It is important to recognize that achieving success academically is as important as acquiring strong character. The priority to focus on producing high achieving students by educational institutions may come at a cost of not focusing on the type of character the students being produced have. The father or male surrogate provides a strong basis for the development of strong character. The inference that to overcome the racial divide we must close the academic gap between whites and blacks is an inaccurate response to a larger issue of how to close the gap between academic success rates amongst these ethnic groups. A possible solution could be to identify what support and awareness teachers and community leaders need to possess to support African-American students with fathers or without them. James A. Banks' study "Cultural Diversity and Education" in a 2006 introduces five phases of multicultural education that should be integrated into the United States educational system that could lead to the support needed. These five phases would give educators and community leaders a blueprint that would enable the development and understanding of curriculum and teaching methods that would better support minority learning. Banks' Phase IV Multicultural Education addresses this specific need by explaining the sense of pride and racial identification that would take place with these or similar positive historical facts taught in the schools could lead to a progressive attitude for African-American students during their school experience, leading to better relationship development with teachers and peers. Those students who are unsuccessful academically and do not have a father or male surrogate need to have their educator aware of the impact that it has on their perception of their personal identity, academic self concept, social sensitivity, race theory, resilience, and vision of success. Fathers and male surrogates across the six dimensions provide academically successful students with the ability to counter negative perceptions found in many media outlets and instructors they encounter. Fathers and male surrogates also provide academically unsuccessful female students with an understanding of how to overcome racial barriers and succeed in creating a better view of self. Academically successful students without a father or male surrogate used outside influences to counter negative perceptions they may encounter. RF12, an academically successful student without a father or male surrogate states, " I hung out with people older than me who took me under their wing and they may not literally know more about a subject than I did but knew more about life...and it helped me out."

Conclusion

Personal Identity

Academically successful students with a father or male surrogate at home developed their personal identity as a combination of not being concerned with the perception others had about them and not comparing themselves to others academically. They use high academic achievement in school to identify who they are. For example, NB9 states,

> Just like you have to be the best at what you do...like my father, too, he's like, you have to be the best in the class against all these people, you have to be No. 1. So, you have to strive for excellence, you don't want to be normal, you have to stand out.

Academically unsuccessful students identify themselves by pursuing activities that bring them personal fulfillment and do not concern themselves primarily with academic achievement as a goal in school. CH7 states, "Finding out one thing that you really like or love and doing it no matter what anybody tells you… success is when you find happiness doing something you love."

CH7 explains further how her father influenced her personal identity when she states, "He was unhappy with his job. He would've rather been doing music and now he's doing music…he's finally finding some type of success because he's enjoying himself."

The difference between academically successful students and academically unsuccessful students' personal identity is the different experience the father or male surrogate had and how he explains that experience to his son or daughter.

John Ogbu and Signithia Fordham's study "Black Students' School Success: Coping with the Burden of "Acting White" in 1986 discuss two parts that contribute to one's personal identity and the responses that develop by minority students in a predominantly white setting. Historically, external forces such as school environment, media depiction of African-Americans, and how the community views your race contribute to the formation of one's personal identity. KF1 describes himself as a "dark-skinned African-American who is very determined." Though he is an academically successful student, he is aware of the way his complexion may be viewed negatively by his peers and instead of hiding it embraces it with pride. William E. Cross' "Shades of

Black" in 1991 Internalization-Commitment fifth stage of racial identity development is characterized by their "personal sense of Blackness into a plan of action or a general sense of commitment." KF1 maintains his connections with black peers, willing to establish meaningful relationships with whites who acknowledge and are respectful of his self-definition as a dark-skinned African-American who is self-determined. However, he does not relinquish his acknowledgment that his complexion plays a role in the way he is judged and is not willing to compromise himself for the purposes of succeeding academically or socially.

Academically successful students with a father or male surrogate present were racially socialized to the world around them and being a high achiever was a character trait their father or male surrogate embedded in them. Academically unsuccessful male students without a father or male surrogate demonstrate a lack of confidence in their ability to compete academically with other students. The negative depiction of African- Americans by the media combined with stereotypes that some professors associated with academically unsuccessful African-American students contributes to their personal identity. Academically unsuccessful female students with a father or male surrogate identify themselves not by academic success but through how happy the choices make them. Their personal identity comes from making choices that are defined by decisions that they make and not by external influences or measurements of success. Academically unsuccessful students did not indicate academic drive. Claude M. Steele's "A Threat in the Air: How Stereotypes Shape Intellectual Identity and Performance" explains that this is due to the lack of perception that one has the skills and resources to prosper. A father or male surrogate provides confidence that any goal is attainable through hard work despite negative depictions by news outlets or negative stereotypes by professors. They also establish that what makes a person successful does not necessarily have to be academic achievement. To the contrary, students without a father or male surrogate may succumb to pathological beliefs that African-American students are not able to achieve high standards academically and adopt the theory that if they can't compete academically they can't achieve success.

Academic Self-Concept

Academically successful students with a father or male surrogate have a high level of confidence in their academic abilities. Academically successful male students with a father in the home or a male surrogate demonstrated how resiliency contributed to their academic success and how they compared their academic abilities to other ethnic groups. "Context, Self, and Action: a Motivational Analysis of Self-system Processes across

Life Span" by James P. Connell and James G. Wellborn in 1990 and "Academic Self-concept and Educational Attainment Level: a Ten-year Longitudinal Study" by Frederic Guay, Simon Larose, and Michael Bovin in 2004 support the findings of this study that a positive family structure that encourages a student's ability to succeed academically will lead to success academically and socially. Herbert Marsh and Rhonda G. Craven's "Reciprocal Effects of Self-concept and Performance from a Multidimensional Perspective: Beyond Seductive Pleasure and Unidimensional" in 1997 believed that socio-economic structure and family structure influenced academic self-concept. The findings from this study demonstrated that academically successful students with a father or male surrogate were not concerned about socio economic status of another person when competing for academic excellence. They were instilled with the idea that they are able to compete on any level academically despite someone's socio-economic status. In many instances, being more successful academically than a person deemed to have more financial support and resources is confirmation that they can accomplish anything. PG4 explains,

> So, when I get a compliment from somebody outside my race that is supposedly doing better financially or academically than I am, it's a shot to do more and it makes me stand on high because I could do better than you.

Own Race Theory

Academically successful students with a father or male surrogate at home developed their own race theory as a combination of understanding how certain instructors may view them and how their culture contributes to their views about race. Academically successful students with a father or male surrogate in the home viewed negative perceptions teachers had of them not as a distraction, but fueled their ambition to do well. Dorinda Carter in 2008 explored how some academically successful students maintain academic success by developing an understanding about race and the barriers that may be placed upon them. They develop adaptive strategies that enable them to navigate successfully through the schooling process that later they can use in life. Prudence L. Carter's "Straddling Boundaries: Identity, Culture, and School" in 2006 explains that the students with the best balance are referred to as "cultural straddlers." They are able to succeed in hostile environments and still maintain cultural ties within their own community. Though the research literature aligns itself with some of the findings in the current study, it does not explore the significance the father's role in developing one's own race theory. The academically successful students with a father or male surrogate showed more willingness to "cultural straddle" than academically unsuccessful students without a father or male surrogate.

Social Sensitivity

Academically successful students with a father or male surrogate describe the development of their social sensitivities as an opportunity to learn from different ethnic groups about an academic subject they may not be strong in. They are confident enough to approach students not in their ethnic group to share and learn about a particular academic subject. Alberto Carbera, Amaury Nora, Patrick Terenzini, Ernest Pascarella, and Linda Hagedorn's "Campus Racial Climate and the Adjustment of Students to College: a Comparison between White Students and African-American Students" in 1999 study regards parental encouragement as a key factor in enabling African-American students aspirations, decision to persist, and the ability to socialize in a predominantly white environment. Academically successful students develop strategies and are encouraged by parents that academic success is not white property. Rather, it becomes what goals you set for yourself and accomplishing those goals no matter what obstacles or ethnicity you are.

Academically unsuccessful students resist exploring relationships with students outside their ethnicity because of the fear of rejection and because of their academic shortcomings. Mendoza Denton, Rodolfo Downey, Valerie Davis, Geraldine Purdie, and Janina Pietrzak's "Research Sensitivity to Status-based

Rejection: Implications for African-American Students in College" in 2002 found that preexisting anxious expectation of race-based rejection play a formative role in African-American college students in a predominantly white environment. They found it leads to a difference in the quality of inter-group relationships and goal realization. African-American students would perceive that their race was viewed negatively by peers and teachers. Academically unsuccessful students in this study without a father or male surrogate demonstrated this exact perception. EB3, an academically successful student who has a father present states, "I like keep around friends that help me build up my academic life. … It's like we share each others ideas and grades." Fathers or male surrogates demonstrate the importance of surrounding yourself with individuals that will encourage your academic success and they provide reasons why this can lead to academic success. JJ2, an academically unsuccessful student without a father or male surrogate explains, "I feel a little intimidated with other races…. I have allowed that to hold me back many times…. I think if he would've raised me to be a fighter if I had that [father] influence." The father or male surrogate instills in their child the importance of surrounding yourself with individuals that will support your academic success, and encourage developing relationships outside of their ethnicity.

Resilience

Academically successful students with a father or male surrogate describe their resiliency as a combination of overcoming a negative perception an instructor may have of them as African-American students, showing that the negative depiction of African- Americans by the media does not apply to them, and not using personal hurdles to distract them from achieving academic success. Dorinda Carter in a 2005 study explains that a student with strong racial pride and heightened sensitivity to negative intellectual stereotypes take on a "prove them wrong" attitude in the classroom where those stereotypes exist. Carter does not address the effect that these negative stereotypes play in the development of academically unsuccessful students' resilience. The data in this study provides that academically unsuccessful students without a father or male surrogate give up on academics because they feel the career goals endorsed by the media and negative perception by their instructors will prevent them from acquiring their goals. Kevin Cokley and Paula Moore's study "Moderating and Mediating Effects of Gender and Psychological Disengagement on the Academic Achievement of African-American College Students" in 2007 suggested that academically unsuccessful students quit in anticipation of not doing well; it is also known as academic disidentification. The relationship between academic self-concept and resilience becomes very clear. The family support and academic confidence that parents provide to the student has a strong relationship with his or her development of resiliency. Consequently, providing the reason why father or male surrogate students have a higher level of academic self-concept and are able to ignore negative perceptions about African-American students in contrast to students without a father or male surrogate in this study who allow negative perceptions affect the way they view themselves academically.

Vision of Success

Academically successful African-American students with a father or male surrogate describe the development of their vision of success as a combination of many things. They use their academic ability to achieve their goals and use the advice or example their male surrogate or father provides for them as a blueprint for developing their vision of success. Further, and similar to Dorinda Carter's 2005's *In a Sea of White People: Analysis of the Experiences and Behaviors of High Achieving Black Students in a Predominantly White High School* by the Harvard University Press "prove them wrong" attitude, they use the validation they would feel they need to succeed despite the negative perception by the media, instructors, and absent father. Na'ilah Nasir, Amina Jones and Milbury McLaughlin's "What Does

It Mean to Be African-American? Constructions of Race and Academic Identity in an Urban Public High School" in 2008 emphasizes that the history of African-Americans in the United States with an ancestry link to slavery, the struggles through the civil rights movements to obtain equality, and the depiction of African-Americans on television as thugs, disinterested in school, and drug dealers reinforces negative stereotypes of African-Americans as anti-intellectuals. The way these stereotypes are perceived by students play an important part in the belief they can achieve their vision of success. Dr. Janie Victoria Ward's *The Skin We're In* in 2000 conveys that parents who emphasize pride, self-respect, and the importance of high levels of achievement as a member of a sub-dominant racial group help the students develop strategies to overcome negative stereotypes. In this research, academically unsuccessful students without a father or male surrogate felt that the lack of a father or male surrogate contributed to a lack of focus and assertiveness. Carla O'Connor in "Dispositions toward (Collective) Struggle and Educational Resilience in the Inner City: a Case Analysis of Six African-American High School Students" in 1997 found that blacks who did not have examples of black role models who overcame barriers to succeed in their own lives had difficulty overcoming constraints and developing a positive vision of their own success. Academically successful males with a father not present in the home but a male surrogate present use the absence of the father as inspiration to succeed and to ultimately make sure they do not repeat the cycle when they become fathers. In contrast, academically unsuccessful males with a father not present in the home but a male surrogate present blame their absent father for their character flaws they feel are too great to overcome and do not use that as inspiration to overcome barriers. This disparity can be due to the role a male surrogate plays in the absence of the father.

Themes Emerging across Dimensions

Similar themes appeared in other dimensions that resulted in there being a correlation between certain themes as it related to certain dimensions.

Academically successful students with a father or male surrogate view of self contributed to the development of the dimensions of academic self-concept and personal identity. The confidence a father or male surrogate instills in their children directly affects the influence on how they view themselves academically and how they identify themselves personally. Academically successful students demonstrated that their father or male surrogate influenced their personal identity. NB9 states, "Well, a big part of it is that I'm half-Panamanian so my father's heritage…that plays a big role because that's where I find a lot of my true identity." NB9 demonstrates that her father's cultural identity played an important part in her personal identity despite it making up only half of her cultural background.

Academically unsuccessful students with or without a father cultural identity contributed to the development of the dimensions of personal identity and academic self-concept. Academically unsuccessful students did not identify their success or happiness based on academic achievement. Academically unsuccessful students did not indicate cultural identity. VR11 said, "For the most part I find my own way.... You know, in a Caribbean family like your mom or your parents don't really want to talk about certain things other than that not much." VR11 expresses the negative contribution his culture has given him and does not take being from the Caribbean as positive.

Academically successful and unsuccessful students with a father or male surrogate's adaptation contributed to the development of personal identity and social sensitivity dimensions. Academically successful and unsuccessful students both adapt but for different reasons. Academically successful students adapt for academic achievement and academically unsuccessful students adapt because of similar interests.

Academically successful and unsuccessful students indicated influence by their father or male surrogate to adapt.

EB3, an academically successful female student explains, "I'm kind of diverse because I have friends that are Hispanic. That are Muslims. And I don't really look at it in that way, just African=American." VH6, an academically unsuccessful male explains, "I don't think the academics have that much an effect on me in the street. I started speaking slang with my friends. Then, I started college and learned those words and stuff...yunno, people start now he goes to school and talks white." Adaptation is used by academically successful male and female students. The difference is what goal they are adapting for and the influence the adaptation has on their academic achievement. Academically successful students adapt for the academic benefits and academically unsuccessful students prefer to adapt in a way that will not allow their peers to see them show any deviation from cultural identity that would label them as "selling out" or acting white.

Academically successful students with a father or male surrogate's resilience contributed to the development of resilience and academic self-concept. Academically successful students with a father or male surrogate were given the confidence by their father or male surrogate that they are able to compete academically with anyone and that the negative perceptions are going to be there, but they must work hard and ignore the negative stereotypes.

Academically successful females did not indicate resilience. Academically successful male students indicated the influence a father or male surrogate had on their resilience. NB9, an academically successful female student with a father states, "Just not letting outside influences influence you on the inside. I need to make sure I am peaceful." DC10, an academically successful male student with a father present explains,

> I played football in high school.... I injured myself and was out of school for a year, so when I came back they didn't transfer my credits, so I was in 12th grade with 10th grade credits. I had to redo high school. I had to do a lot to get out on time

The female student was more concerned about her inner peace and being able to make decisions that she made on her own without reacting to outside influences. The academically successful student demonstrates resiliency as a way to overcome academic hurdles that may prevent his pursuit of academic excellence.

Recommendations

Universities and professors need to develop a training program for new teachers that would focus on understanding how teachers may bring race bias views into the classroom without realizing it. Educators must develop programs that initiate father or male surrogate involvement in the development of a student's academic path. Fathers and male surrogates must realize the importance of being a part of their children's lives and lessons they have learned that must be passed down to their sons or daughters to demonstrate that negative perceptions and stereotypes by media, professors, and community do not define who they are or can become. The influence that a father or male surrogate has must be realized by the father or male surrogate as an influence that transcends academic achievement and has the ability to contribute to the development of human character.

Producers of media outlets and media moguls must be more responsible when portraying images of African-American families. The use of creating the pathological idea of single mothers and dead-beat fathers must stop. African-American family structure may not resemble white family structures but they do have an internal support structure that enables high academic achievement and strong character development that in some instance surpasses white family structures. The measurement of success in educational institutions is academic, which the media, professors, and community view as success. However, African-Americans academic success and strong character is not portrayed enough. The worth of an individual should not be grounded in academic achievement alone.

Recommendations for Future Research

One research recommendation is to have a longitudinal study to see how the academically successful and unsuccessful African-American students with a father or male surrogate present influenced their career paths versus not having a father or male surrogate present. This would enable the researcher to measure if high academics and a father or male surrogate present or a father or male surrogate not present influences a successful career path.

A second research recommendation is to conduct a study that examines the mother's influence on the development of personal identity, social sensitivity, own race theory, academic self-concept, resilience, and vision of success in academically successful and unsuccessful students with a mother, male surrogate or neither a mother nor male surrogate present.

A third research recommendation is to apply this study using other ethnic groups to determine the influence a father or male surrogate may have on the six dimensions.

A fourth research recommendation is to conduct a study on the "ghost father" concept. This would determine how an absent father still influences his child's development of the six dimensions in this study.

References

Abdul-Adil, J. K., & Farmer, A. D. J. (2006). Inner-city African-American parental involvement in elementary schools: Getting beyond urban legends of apathy. School Psychology Quarterly, 21(1), 1–12.

Amatea, E. S., Smith-Adcock, S., & Villares, E. (2006). From family deficit to family strength: Viewing families' contributions to children's learning from a family resilience perspective. Professional School Counseling, 9, 177-188.

American Psychological Association. (2001) Publication manual (5th Fifth Edition), Washington D.C.: American Psychological Association.

Aschenbrenner, J.(1973). Extended families among Black Americans. Journal of Comparative Studies. Vol.4.

Awad, H. G., (2007) The Role of Racial Identity, Academic Self-concept, and Self-Esteem in the Prediction of Academic Outcomes for African-American Students. Journal of Black Psychology Vol.33, No.2, 188-207.

Banks, J.A., (2006) Cultural Diversity and Education: Foundations Curriculum and Teaching (5th ed.), Boston: Pearson.

Bernard, B. (1991). Fostering resiliency in kids: Protective factors in the family, school, and community. Portland, OR: Northwest Regional Educational Laboratory.

Boyd-Franklin, N. (1985). A psycho-educational perspective on Black parenting. In H.P. McAdoo and J.L. McAdoo(Eds.) Black Children,(pp.195-209).CA: SagePub.

Bryant-Williams, W. and Fannin, R. (1996). Middle-Class African-American Perceptions Regarding Their Strengths. Annual Conference of the National Council on Family Relations.

Carbera, A. F., Nora, A., Terenzini, T. P., Pascarella, E., Hagedorn, S. L., (1999) Campus Racial Climate and the Adjustment of Students to College. A Comparison between White students and African-American students. The journal of Higher Education Vol. 70 No. 2.

Carter, J. D. (2008) Achievement as Resistance: The Development of a Critical Race Achievement Ideology among Black achievers. Harvard Educational Review.Vol.78, No.3 466-497.

Carter, L. P., (2006) Straddling Boundaries: Identity, Culture, and School. Sociology of Education Vol. 79, 304-328.

Carter , J.D. (2005) In a Sea of White people: Analysis of the experiences and behaviors of high-achieving Black students in a predominantly White high school. Harvard University, Cambridge, MA.

Cokley, K., (2000) An Investigation of Academic Self-Concept and its Relationship to Academic Achievement in African-American College Students. Vol.26, No.2, 148-164.

Cokley, K., & Moore, P., (2007) Moderating and Mediating Effects of Gender and Psychological Disengagement on the Academic Achievement of African-American College Students. Journal of Black Psychology Vol. 33, No.2 169-187.

Coley, L. R. (2003). Daughter-Father Relationships and Adolescent Psychosocial Functioning in Low-Income African-American Families. Journal of Marriage and Family. Vol.65, No.4.

Connell, J. P. (1990). Context, self, and action: A motivational analyses of self-system processes across the life-span. In. D. Cicchetti & M. Beeghly (Eds.), The self in transaction: Infancy to childhood (pp. 61-97). Chicago, IL: University of Chicago Press.

Cross, W.E. Jr. (1971) The Negro-to-Black conversion experience. Black Word, 20(9), 13-27.

Deton, R. M., Downey, G., Davis, A., Purdie, V., Pietrzak (2002) Sensitivity to Status Based: Rejection: Implications for African-American Students College Experience. Journal of Personality and Social Psychology Vol. 83 No. 4, 896-918.

Delgado, R. (1995) Critical race theory: The cutting edge. Philadelphia: Temple University Press.

Delgado, R. & Stefancic, J. (2001).Critical race theory: An introduction. New York; New York University Press.

Delgado-Gaitan, C., & Trueba, H. (1991) Crossing cultural borders: Education for immigrant families in America. New York: Falmer.

Dowling College. (2005) Style & publication manual for all proposals & dissertations. Dowling College, School of

Ebaugh, H., Curry, M. (2000) Fictive Kinship as Social Capital in New Immigrant Communities. Sociological Perspectives Vol. 43 No. 2, 189-209.

Evans, M.D.R., J. Kelley, and R.A. Wanner. 2001. Educational attainment of the children of divorce: Australia, 1940–1990. Journal of Sociology 37(3):275–297.

Flowers, L., Milner, H., & Moore, J. (2003). Effects of Locus of Control on African-American High School Seniors'

Educational Aspirations: Implications for Preservice and Inservice High School Teachers and Counselors. High School Journal, 87(1), 39-50.

Floyd, C. (1996) Achieving despite the odds: A study of resilience among a group of African-American high school seniors. Journal of Negro Education Vol. 65, No.2 181-189.

Fordham, S. (1988) Racelessness as a factor in Black students' success: pragmatic strategy or pyrrhic victory? Harvard Educational Review, Vol. 58 No.1, 54-84.

Gay, G. (2000). Culturally responsive teaching: Theory, research, & practice. New York: Teachers College Press.

Gutman, L. M, & McLoyd, V. C. (2000). Parents' management of their children's education within the home, at school, and in the community: An examination of African-American families living in poverty. Urban Review, 32, 1-24.

Guay, F., Larose, S., & Boivin, M. (2004). Academic self-concept and educational attainment level: A ten-year longitudinal study. Self and Identity, 3, 53–68.

Hammer, J. (1997) The fathers of "fatherless" Black children. Families in Society: Journal Of Contemporary Human Services.

Hill, R.B. (1972) The strength of Black Families. New York: Emerson Hall Publisher.

Johnson, D. (1996). Father Presence Matters: A Review of the Literature National Center on Fathers and Families.

Katz, W.A. (1973) The Strength of black Families, by Robert A. Hill: A Review. National Center for Research and Information on Equal Education Opportunity. Columbia University. New York, New York.

Lessing, E. E., Zagorin, S. W., & Nelson, D. (1970). WISC subtest and IQ score correlates of father absence. Journal of Genetic Psychology, 117, 181-195.

Logan, S. (1983). Fathers as Nurturers. Sociological Abstracts No.P5, 718 (New York): Chicago University Press.

Marsh, Herbert W.; Craven, Rhonda G. (2006) Reciprocal Effects of Self-Concept and Performance From a Multidimensional Perspective: Beyond Seductive Pleasure and Unidimensional. Perspectives Perspectives on Psychological Science, Volume 1, Number 2, 133-163.

Marsh, H. W., & O'Neill, R. (1984). Self-Description Questionnaire III (SDQIII): The construct validity of multidimensional self-concept ratings by late adolescents. Journal of Educational Measurement, 21, 153–174.

McAdoo, J.L. (1986). The roles of African-American fathers in the socialization of the children. In H.P. McAdoo. Black Families,(pp.183-197). CA: Sage Publications.

Mehta, Sejal., Sanders, T., Goodman, R., (2007) Recommendations for Working with African-American Parents of Primary School Children in Low-resourced Schools.

Mickelson, A. R. (1981) Black Working Class Adolescents' Attitudes Toward Academic Achievement. American Educational Research Association.

Milne, A.M., Myers, D.E., Rosenmthal, A.S., Ginsbburg, A.(1986) Single parent, working mothers, and the educational achievement of school children. Sociology of education, 59(3), 125-139.

Nasir, Na'ilah Suad, McLaughlin, Milbrey W., Jones, Amina (2008) What Does It Mean to Be African-American? Constructions of Race and Academic Identity in an Urban Public High School American Educational Research Journal 2009 46: 73-114.

Obetz, W. (1987) A Proposed Model for Categorizing Successful and Non-Successful Student Outcomes at CCP. Office of Institutional Research.

O'Connor, C. (1997). Dispositions toward (collective) struggle and educational resilience in the inner city: A case analysis of six African –American high school students. American Educational Research Journal, 34(4), 593-629.

Ogbu, J. & U Fordham, S. (1986). Black students' school success: Coping with the "burden of 'acting White." The Urban Review, 18(3), 176-206.

Ogbu, J.(2004). Collective Identity and the Burden of " Acting White" in Black History, Community, and Education. The Urban Review, Vol. 36, No.1.

Ogbu, J.(1981) Schooling in the Ghetto: An Ecological Perspective on Community & Home Influence. National Institute of Education.

Ogbu, J. (1978). Minority education and caste. New York: Academic Press.

Patterson, Orlando (1982) Slavery and social death: A comparative study. Harvard University Press.

Perry T. (2003) Achieving in post- Civil Rights America: the outline of a theory. In T. Perry, C. Steele, & A.G. Hilliard (Eds.) Young, gifted and Black: Promoting high achievement among African-American students(pp.87-108) Boston, MA: Beacon Press.

Robinson, T., Ward, T. (1991) A belief in self far greater than anyone's belief: Cultivating resistance among African-American female adolescents, New York: Hawthorn, pp. 87-103.

Roithymayr, D. (1999). Introduction to critical race theory in educational research and praxis In I,. Parker, D. Deyhle, & s. Villenas(Eds.) Race is ... race isn't : Critical race theory and qualitative studies in education(pp.1-6) Boulder ,Co: Western Press.

Seccombe, K. (2002). Improving the Odds Vs. Changing the Odds: Resiliency in Poor Families. Journal of Marriage and the Family.

Seidman, I.E. (1998) Interviewing as qualitative research: guide for researchers in education and the social sciences(2nd ed.). New York: Teachers College Press.

Sellers, R.M., Chavous, T. M., & Cooke, D. Y. (1998) Racial ideology and racial centrality as predictors of African-American college students' academic performance. Journal of Black Psychology, No. 24, Vol. 1, 8-27.

Shavelson, R.J., Hubner, J. , & Stanton, g. (1976) Self – Concept: Validation of construct interpretations. Review of Educational Research, 46, 407-441.

Skowron, E. (2005) Parent differentiation of self and child competence in low-income urban families. Journal of Counseling Psychology Vol.52, No.3 337-346.

Smith-Maddox, R. (1999). The social networks and resources of African-American eighth graders: Evidence from the national education longitudinal study of 1988, Adolescence, 34, 169-183.

Steele, C.M. (1997) A threat in the Air: How stereotypes shape intellectual identity and performance. American Psychologist. Vol. 52 613-629.

Taylor, K.A, Kowalski, P. (2004) Naïve Psychological Science: The Prevalence, Strength, And Sources Of Misconception. The Psychological Record No.54 15-25l

Thompson, M., Alexander, K., & Entwisle, D. (1988) Household composition parental expectations, and school achievement. Social Forces, 66, 424-451.

Tutweiler, S.W. (2005) Teachers as collaborative partners: Working with diverse families and communities. Mahwah, NJ: Erlbaum.

Vandiver, B. J., Cross, W. E., Jr., Worrell, F. C., & Fhagen-Smith, P. E. (2002) Validating the Cross Racial Identity Scale. Journal of counseling Psychology Vol. 49, No.1 71-85.

Ward, J.V. (2000) The skin we're in: Teaching our children to be emotionally strong, socially smart, spiritually connected. New York: Free Press.

Woodson, G.C. (1972) The Mis-Education of the Negro. Dover African-American Bks.

About the Author

Dr. A'lon Michael Holliday was born on Long Island, New York to proud parents Marguertie and William Holliday. He was educated at Lasalle Military Academy and received his Bachelors of Science from Boston College in Philosophy and Political Science. He later Attended C.W. Post Long Island University and received his Masters in Public Administration. Due to his fascination with law and public policy he pursued his law degree at Thomas M. Cooley Law School. As he returned home and began to see the need for African American male leadership in education he attended Dowling College where he obtained his Doctorate in Educational Administration focusing on African American Family structures.

He currently resides in Atlanta with his Wife, Tiffany and his two children Kailen and Siena. He is a member of the Dekalb Chapter of the 100 Black Men. He enjoys traveling and spending time with his family.

Few studies examine the role fathers play in the development of their African-American child's academic achievement, despite the growing body of research on the role mothers play on their students' achievement. To fill this gap, this present study of *Father and Child* examines how the father or male surrogate influences the development of African-American students in the six dimensions of personal identity, social sensitivity, academic self-concept, resilience, race theory, and vision of own success. The results examined in this book indicate differences between academically successful African-American students with a father or male surrogate and academically unsuccessful students without such a role model.

www.ingramcontent.com/pod-product-compliance
Lightning Source LLC
Chambersburg PA
CBHW071449080526
44587CB00014B/2046